HERBAL ACTIVITIES FOR KIDS

50 NATURE CRAFTS, RECIPES, AND GARDEN PROJECTS

Molly Meehan Brown and Friends

Storey Publishing

The mission of Storey Publishing is to serve our customers by
publishing practical information that encourages
personal independence in harmony with the environment.

Edited by Diana Rupp and Liz Bevilacqua

Art direction and book design by Jessica Armstrong

Text production by Jennifer Jepson Smith

Back cover and interior illustrations by © Madison Safer

Front cover collage by © Martin O'Neill/Cut it
    Out Studio, using images by © Aylén Maquehue,
    © Bogdan Sonjachnyj/Shutterstock.com,
    © Butterfly Hunter/Shutterstock.com, Mars Vilaubi
    © Storey Publishing, © Sveta Lagutina/Shutterstock
    .com, © VLADIMIR VK/Shutterstock.com
Back cover photography by © FotoHelin/Shutterstock
    .com, t.c.; Mars Vilaubi © Storey Publishing, t.l. & b.c.;
    © Molly Meehan Brown, b.l. & b.r.; © sumi dutta, t.r.
Interior photography by © Amanda Hutchison, 43, 96 t.l.;
    © Angela Bakr (Rahim), 97 b.r.; © Arvolyn Hill, 95 b.r.;
    © Aylén Maquehue, 30, 31, 69 b.l., 69 b.r., 96 b.l.; © Ayo
    Ngozi, courtesy of Molly Meehan Brown, 71, 97 m.l.;
    © DisobeyArt/Shutterstock.com, 16 girl; © FotoHelin/
    Shutterstock.com, 76; Courtesy of Geoffrey Edwards,
    Grain & Pestle, 95 m.r.; Courtesy of Irlanda (Landis)
    Pulido, 97 t.r.; © Kate Johnson, 25 b.l, 25 t., 95 t.l.;
    © Kuttelvaserova Stuchelova/Shutterstock.com, 14 r.;
    © Lauren Lupo Passero, 97 b.l.; © Lev Kropotov/
    Shutterstock.com, 20; © Lipatova Maryna/Shutterstock
    .com, 25 b.r.; © Madison McCoy, 96 b.r.; © MarcoFood/
    Shutterstock.com, 14 l.; Mars Vilaubi © Storey
    Publishing, 8, 9, 11 all but t., 12, 13, 16 art on
    paper, 16 b., 17, 21, 22, 54, 59, 62, 65, 67 flowers, 68,
    69 c., 69 t.; Courtesy of Marysia Miernowska & Ira
    Christian of School of the Sacred Wild, 97 t.l.;
    © Molly Meehan Brown, 3, 11 t., 38, 39, 72, 75, 99;
    © Namita Kulkarni, 96 m.l.; © New Africa/Shutterstock
    .com, 33; Courtesy Rebecca Cecere Seward, 98 b.l.;
    Samaria Marley, 73; © sumi dutta, 63, 64, 95 t.r.;
    Courtesy of Suzanna Stone, 98 t.r.; © Tamara Kulikova/
    Shutterstock.com, 15 l.; © Tim UR/Shutterstock
    .com, 15 r.; Courtesy of Toni Roberts, 66, 67 m., 67 t.,
    98 t.l.; © Zenovia D'Arienzo and family, 95 b.l.

Text © 2024 by Molly Meehan

Storey books may be purchased in bulk for
business, educational, or promotional use. Special
editions or book excerpts can also be created to
specification. For details, please contact your local
bookseller or the Hachette Book Group Special Markets
Department at special.markets@hbgusa.com.

Storey Publishing
210 MASS MoCA Way
North Adams, MA 01247
storey.com

Storey Publishing is an imprint of Workman
Publishing, a division of Hachette Book Group, Inc.,
1290 Avenue of the Americas, New York, NY 10104.
The Storey Publishing name and logo are registered
trademarks of Hachette Book Group, Inc.

Distributed in Europe by Hachette Livre, 58 rue
Jean Bleuzen, 92 178 Vanves Cedex, France
Distributed in the United Kingdom by Hachette
Book Group, UK, Carmelite House, 50 Victoria
Embankment, London EC4Y 0DZ

ISBNs: 978-1-63586-584-4 (paperback);
978-1-63586-585-1 (ebook)

Printed in China by R. R. Donnelley on
paper from responsible sources
10   9   8   7   6   5   4   3   2   1

RRD-S

Library of Congress Cataloging-in-Publication Data on file

To my children, my Papi, my siblings, parents,
family, teachers, and community of dear friends and
fellow herbalists: I love you and am thankful to you.

To our community of Young Ones:
We see you, we hope to share with you the best of
what we've got, to learn from you, do better for you,
and help you lead the way. You are hope,
you are every possibility!

CONTENTS

Welcome. vi

Introduction to the World of Herbs 1

CHAPTER 1
See and Investigate

Nature Mandala 8

Herbal Color Wheel 11

Plant Press and
Herbarium 12

Botanical Illustration 14

Blackberry Ink and
Twig Pen 16

No-Waste Kitchen
Gardening 18

How to Sprout 20

Glass Jar Herb Garden 22

Simple Elderberry
Propagation 24

CHAPTER 2
The Taste of Nature

Luna's Fairy
Berry Tea 29

Party Punch 30

Fire Cider Oxymel 32

Spiced Turmeric
Kale Chips 33

Edible Flower
Ice Cubes 34

Garden-Fresh Lunch 36

Decorative Herbal
Pizzas 38

Chickweed Pesto 39

Rundown Stew 40

Hot Summer Day
Ice Pops 42

Pistachio–Goji
Berry Chocolate 43

Coconut Drops 44

Wild Berry Crumble 46

CHAPTER 3

Sweet and Spicy Smells

Rosemary
Water Mist 50

Elderberry Herbal
Syrup 51

Tummy Trouble Tea 52

Herb and Spice Apple-
Pear Topping 54

Kitchen Wreath 55

Lemon Balm Lip Balm 56

Evergreen Salve 57

Peppermint Glycerite 58

CHAPTER 4

Let's Use Our Hands

Natural Dye
with Turmeric 62

Fresh Herb Cards
and Invitations 65

Pressed Flower Collage 66

Mugwort Dream Portal 68

Leaf Paper 70

Plant Garlands 72

Flower Tape Bracelets 73

Daisy Chain Crown 74

Starting Seeds 76

Seed Balls 78

Dehydrated Harvest 79

CHAPTER 5

Listen, Move, and Rejoice

Seed Rattles 82

Plant Wind Chimes 83

Listening Garden 84

Nature Poem 88

CHAPTER 6

Community Constellation

Little Herbalist
Saves the World! 90

Community of Contributors 95

Gratitude from Molly 99

Resources 101

Index 102

Metric Conversions 105

Welcome

My name is Molly Meehan Brown, and I am so very grateful that you are here to learn about herbs! I am an herbalist, gardener, and mama. We created Wild Ginger Community Herbal Center and Kids Herbalism as a place to build relationships between plants, the land, and people.

We are honored to share our home and the land we live on with our community as an intergenerational gathering place, a space of joy and connection, where we can all share and exchange knowledge.

COMMUNITY AND CREATIVITY

I gathered this very special community of educators, artists, gardeners, farmers, botanists, and herbalists from all over the world to contribute activities, recipes, knowledge, and passion for plants to share with kids. (To learn more about the contributors, turn to page 95.) You are going to learn about herbs through the senses. You are going to see, smell, hear, taste, and touch herbs. You are also going to build relationships and community— with the plants and with the people whom you explore the plant world with. I like to think of every activity, project, and recipe in this book as a seed—one that can grow your knowledge of plants and your creative expression.

Feel free to experiment, have fun, and play. The activities here are meant to be practiced by kids and adults, with families and friends. Picture-perfect results are not the goal here. I hope this book helps you cultivate the very special skill of imagination. Imagination helps us see possibilities and solve challenges.

A NOTE FOR GROWN-UPS

Kids may need supportive supervision for some of the activities in this book. Younger ones may need help when using ovens, stoves, knives, and so on. It is also essential to correctly identify wild plants. Some plants are entirely safe; others are potentially dangerous. Always consult with a qualified practitioner for help with identifying and determining the safety of a plant.

DIVERSITY OF ABILITY

A special note for our beloved community members who join us in diversity of ability: These activities are designed to engage multiple senses, and every reader should tune in to our beloved plant kin with the sense of their choosing. For example, if you are vision impaired and want to direct your attention toward touch or hearing with a plant, that is wonderful. The end goal is to grow your relationship with the plant. Sometimes this happens in the most simple ways, just by being in each other's presence.

I am so very thankful you have joined me and my friends here!

In community,

Molly

Introduction to the
WORLD OF HERBS

What Is an Herb?

Any plant used for healing is called an herb. But healing can happen in many forms. Herbs are used not just for physical healing but also as part of our arts, rituals, traditions, and cultural practices. They are used in our food, in sacred and spiritual work, in our clothing and jewelry, and so much more!

Many species across the animal kingdom use herbs for their food and healing. Plants can even help heal each other.

Depending on the plant, we work with different parts of herbs, such as the leaves, roots, flowers, seeds, bark, sap, or stems. Many of us already have abundant herbs in our home; often our kitchen cabinets are full of herbs like rosemary, oregano, black pepper, chile, and thyme.

What Is an Herbalist?

An herbalist is a person who works with plants for healing. There are many ways to be an herbalist. Some herbalists make herbal medicines to help people treat illness and feel healthier, some grow herbs and provide them to the community, and some forage and wildcraft herbs. Others work as herbal clinicians or practitioners, helping people learn how to use herbs to support their health. Some are herbal educators, and others are scientists who work in labs and run studies on herbs.

The herb-infused teas, oils, salves, syrups, and other remedies we use to help support our health and wellness are all called herbal preparations.

Parts of a Plant

FRUIT is not only delicious for humans, animals, and insects, but it also contains seeds.

FLOWERS are the reproductive part of a plant. Their color, scent, or shape often attracts pollinators (see page 84).

SEEDS germinate and create a new plant when combined with water, sunlight, and soil.

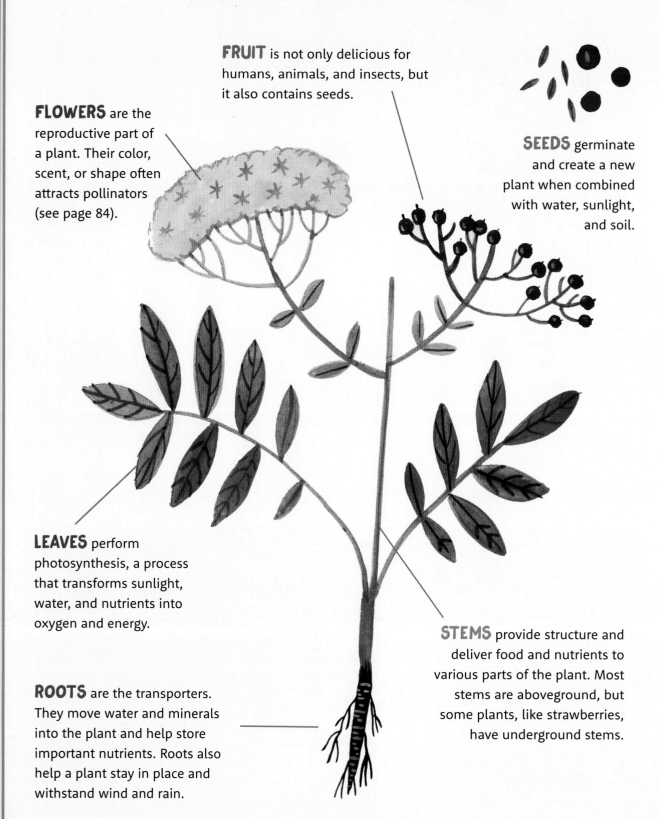

LEAVES perform photosynthesis, a process that transforms sunlight, water, and nutrients into oxygen and energy.

STEMS provide structure and deliver food and nutrients to various parts of the plant. Most stems are aboveground, but some plants, like strawberries, have underground stems.

ROOTS are the transporters. They move water and minerals into the plant and help store important nutrients. Roots also help a plant stay in place and withstand wind and rain.

Plant Names

Did you know that plants have more than one name? Every plant has one scientific name that is used worldwide and usually a few common names as well.

Scientific or botanical names are sometimes called Latin names because they are in the Latin language. Because scientific names are unique to each species, they can help you correctly identify a plant. The first name is always capitalized and identifies the genus that the plant belongs to, while the second part is lowercased and refers to the plant's species. For example, *Lavandula* is the genus lavender, and *angustifolia* is a particular species of lavender plants. The species name often describes an interesting quality about the plant; *angustifolia* means "narrow leaf."

The common name is the name the plant is called in a specific region or place and often reflects the traditional use of a plant. Sneezewort's scientific name is *Achillea ptarmica*. *Achillea* refers to the Greek mythological warrior Achilles, who by legend treated soldiers' wounds with this genus, and *ptarmica* comes from the Greek word *ptairo*, which means "to cause to sneeze." Can you guess what sneezewort was used for? (That's right—to make people sneeze!)

It is important to realize that colonists sometimes gave Latin names to plants that were unfamiliar to them, but that doesn't mean they discovered the plants. In fact, Indigenous communities were often familiar with the plants long before any colonists arrived.

Building Right Relationship

Through the web of life—people, plants, animals, insects, microbes, soils, streams, valleys, mountains, oceans, and everything in between—we are all deeply interconnected. We are part of a system. Each member of this system holds a special gift, a function necessary to the whole. Whether we like it or not, what affects one of us eventually can affect all of us. For example, your decision to plant a community garden will improve the life of the people in your neighborhood, but it will also help butterflies, animals, the soil, and more.

Every day, with every decision we make and action we take, we should try to remember our relationship with this web of life. Herbalists call this "right relationship." Right relationship is rooted in respect, care, gratitude, and love for the life around us.

What a wonderful journey you have begun!

Learning through Your Senses

Each chapter in this book is dedicated to one of your five senses. Directing your attention toward your senses will help you connect with your body and learn from the plants directly. Ask yourself: How does this plant smell? How does this leaf feel? Does this herb taste spicy or sweet? What structures can I see on this plant? How do I feel when I drink this tea?

Your senses can help you identify certain patterns that give clues about a plant's uses. For example, many bitter plants help cool down your body, improve your digestion, and support your liver. Many spicy plants warm up your body and help your body fight off the microbes that can make you sick. Sweet herbs are often nourishing to your body, and sour plants contain high concentrations of vitamin C.

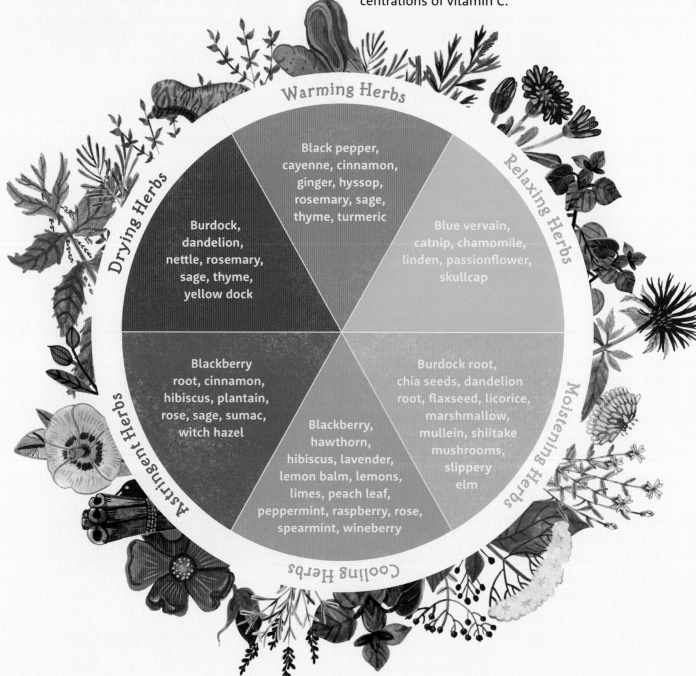

Warming Herbs

Black pepper, cayenne, cinnamon, ginger, hyssop, rosemary, sage, thyme, turmeric

Relaxing Herbs

Blue vervain, catnip, chamomile, linden, passionflower, skullcap

Drying Herbs

Burdock, dandelion, nettle, rosemary, sage, thyme, yellow dock

Blackberry root, cinnamon, hibiscus, plantain, rose, sage, sumac, witch hazel

Astringent Herbs

Blackberry, hawthorn, hibiscus, lavender, lemon balm, lemons, limes, peach leaf, peppermint, raspberry, rose, spearmint, wineberry

Burdock root, chia seeds, dandelion root, flaxseed, licorice, marshmallow, mullein, shiitake mushrooms, slippery elm

Moistening Herbs

Cooling Herbs

How Herbs Affect Your Body

When you eat herbs or use them on your skin, they have certain *energetics*, meaning "actions" or "qualities." Your body also has energetics. The best way to understand herbal energetics is to think of a time when you were sick. Maybe you had a cold, with a sore throat, fever, and dry cough. Your body probably felt hot and dry. In this situation, you could use herbs with a cooling or moistening effect: mint in a soothing tea or slippery elm in a throat lozenge.

Maybe you can remember another time when your chest was congested, you sneezed a lot, and there was snot everywhere! When you have a damp cold with a lot of thick phlegm, you can use herbs that are warming and drying: rosemary, thyme, or cinnamon.

Rather than just thinking about certain herbs as being good for one thing or another, you can get to know which herbs help your body and then match the energetics of your body to the energetics of the plants.

Reflection Activities

As you begin to build your relationship with herbs, it is important to take time to reflect, be still, and listen.

Plant Journey

A plant journey is very simple. Take some quiet time to go and be near a plant that is calling to you. The plant can be in a garden, along a path, in a pot, or anywhere. Sit or lie down, close your eyes, and get comfortable. Begin to tune in to the plant. As you are there with the plant, observe anything that comes up in your mind or body. Maybe you see certain colors or images, or you have certain feelings. Any messages from the plant?

Observing and Drawing

Take the time to look at a plant deeply and draw it in as much detail as you can. Notice every line on the leaf. Are the edges of the leaves smooth or jagged? What is the shape of the stem? Is it woody or not? Does the plant lean in one direction? Toward the sun? Do the leaves have a smooth surface, or do you see tiny hairs? What insects or critters are visiting this plant? Are there any other life-forms growing on it? Paying close attention to a plant can help you notice tiny details in other things around you.

Plant Journaling

You can create your own nature journal to document what you learn, reflect on your experiences, and grow through your herbal journey. You can fill the pages with drawings, press plants and flowers, make notes on herbs, and write about your relationship with plants. When you fill up one journal, start a new one, and save all of your journals in a special place.

CHAPTER 1

SEE AND INVESTIGATE

I see the lavender, the sage,
The chamomile and rue,
The garden full of shapes and sizes,
With flowers of white, yellow, purple, and blue.
I gaze across the meadow,
Filled with echinacea, monarda, and milkweed.
The silver-green grasses dance in the wind.
Imagine all the pollinators they feed!

Walking carefully through the forest now,
I keep an eye to see which friends I'll meet,
Each forest a home for different plants,
Depending where you lay your feet.

The tropical rainforest,
Filled with fungi, roots, and leaves,
So many hold such special medicine,
The story of plants and
people interweave.

Nature
MANDALA

with Arvolyn Hill

Creating a nature mandala helps you be present in and connect to the natural world. The word *mandala* means "circle" in Sanskrit. Buddhist monks have practiced mandala art for thousands of years. Mandalas teach us about symmetry—when an object is exactly the same on one side as it is on the other. Symmetry can be found throughout nature, from a butterfly's wings to the way petals bloom on a flower.

MATERIALS

- **Something to hold found objects, like a bowl, basket, or bag**
- **Scissors (if harvesting)**

NOTE: *If you gather your found objects in a public space, collect plant material that has already fallen to the ground. If you're in your own space or have permission to do so, you can harvest fresh herbs and flowers.*

INSTRUCTIONS

1. Gather some natural objects you like, such as flowers, leaves, twigs, feathers, rocks, and acorns in different sizes, shapes, and colors. Try to find a few of each.

2. Find an open space outdoors. It can be in your yard, on pavement, or on a stump. Pick a space where you think others will be able to enjoy the mandala.

3. Choose an object to be the center of your mandala. It can be big or small. If you found only one of a particular item, then it's perfect for the middle.

4. Arrange more objects around the center in circles or regular spaces that please you. Play around with the sizes, colors, and shapes.

5. When you are done, leave the mandala for others to enjoy. You can come back as often as you wish to see how your mandala changes over time.

When you are done, leave the mandala for others to enjoy.

Garden Meditation

with Madison McCoy

Find a place outside where plants grow, like your yard, a garden, the woods, or a park. If it feels comfy, let's close our eyes for a moment. (If closing eyes doesn't feel right for you, find something around you that makes you feel safe.)

- Begin by taking three deep breaths, feeling the air enter through your nose and exit through your mouth.

- Breathe in (pause for 3 seconds) and breathe out (pause for 3 seconds).

- Breathe in (pause for 3 seconds) and breathe out (pause for 3 seconds).

- Breathe in (pause for 3 seconds) and breathe out (pause for 3 seconds).

Great work!

I invite you to open your eyes if they were closed. Now that our bodies are calm, let's go find a plant that might want to get to know us better.

Once you have found your special plant friend, introduce yourself! Say, "Hey! My name is _____, and I'm so excited to meet you."

Looking at the plant, take another deep breath, and imagine your heart is making a glowing bubble of light that surrounds you and the plant. This is a place where you and your new plant friend can communicate. Ask your plant friend:

- Who are you? What is your name?

- How do you like to help people?

- How can you help me with something that is hard in my life?

- Do you have a message you want to share with me?

Maybe the answers don't make sense, but maybe they do! Either way, you can trust what you're hearing in your heart. Your connection with plants is ancient. Taking one more deep breath, tell your plant friend, "Thank you for our amazing adventure today. I will try to visit again soon." Give them a high five, a fist bump, or a little dance to close the meditation.

Herbal COLOR WHEEL

with Molly Meehan Brown

Creating a color wheel is a fun way to connect with plants and notice the incredible array of colors that exist in nature.

MATERIALS

- Piece of white paper
- Bowl, no bigger than your paper
- Pencil or pen
- Ruler
- Paint, markers, colored pencils, or crayons
- Plant materials (leaves, flowers, seeds, and so on)

INSTRUCTIONS

1. Put your piece of paper on a flat surface. Set the bowl upside down on the paper. Using a pencil or pen, trace around it to draw a circle.

2. Using the ruler, divide the circle into equal parts, like a pie. The more sections you divide the wheel into, the more colors you can use.

3. Fill in each section of the wheel with a different color. You can color a basic rainbow palette (red, orange, yellow, green, blue, purple) or use colors that match your plant materials more closely.

4. Arrange your plant materials in groups around each color.

PLANT PRESS
and Herbarium

with Suzanna Stone

A plant press preserves flowers and leaves while keeping their shape, color, and vibrancy. A fun way to get to know what grows around you is to make an herbarium or ID guide from plants that you gather and press.

MATERIALS

FOR YOUR PLANT PRESS

- Scissors
- Medium-weight cardboard
- Watercolor paper
- Two 7 x 9-inch pieces of plywood for covers
- Two 1-inch-wide x 20-inch-long hook-and-loop straps

FOR YOUR HERBARIUM

- Tweezers
- Craft glue
- Heavyweight paper
- Pen or pencil, for labeling
- Folder, for storing pages

The cardboard and watercolor pages of the press help the plants dry faster.

INSTRUCTIONS

The Plant Press

1. Cut two to five cardboard rectangles and at least two pieces of the watercolor paper to the same size as the cover.

2. Prepare the press by layering sheets of paper and cardboard. Start with cardboard, add two sheets of paper, and then top with cardboard. Continue as desired.

3. Add the covers and secure with the straps.

The Herbarium

1. Harvest a variety of flowers and leaves on a dry day. Take notes as you gather to add later.

2. Open the press to the bottom layer of cardboard and the first sheet of watercolor paper. Arrange plants in a single layer on the watercolor paper, making sure they don't touch. Cover with a second piece of watercolor paper. Place a piece of cardboard on top.

3. Repeat as desired.

4. Secure the straps around the plant press tightly. Dry for 2 to 3 weeks.

5. Carefully remove the top sheet of watercolor paper. Use tweezers to gently remove the dried plants.

6. Glue each plant to heavyweight paper and label with a pen or pencil.

7. Store your herbarium in a folder with pieces of paper between each page, or laminate the pages to make the herbarium even more durable.

When the plant pieces are completely dry, they will be as thin as tissue paper.

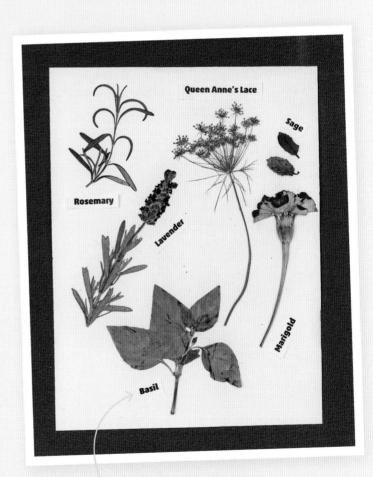

Label each plant and add any other notes or information you have learned about the plant.

Botanical
ILLUSTRATION

with Namita Kulkarni

In this activity, we will observe and then draw mint, pansy, rose, and dill, but you can choose any plants you like.

MATERIALS

- Paper
- Pencil
- Colored pencils
- Ruler (optional)

- Kneaded eraser, for erasing pencil lines, as needed
- Mint, pansy, rose, and dill cuttings or photographs

Mint

Mint is one of the most well-loved herbs. It gets its name from a Greek mythological character named Menthe. One of its Spanish names is yerba buena, or "good herb." Ancient Egyptian medical texts from as far back as 1550 BCE mention mint.

Pansy

Pansies grow well in cooler climates and are known to be hardy, disease-resistant plants. They get their name from the French word *pensée*, meaning "thought" or "remembrance."

INSTRUCTIONS

1. Set out a piece of paper, your art materials, and the plant you want to draw.

2. Look at your herb closely before beginning to draw. Squint to see its basic shape.

3. Start to look back and forth from the item to your paper, using a pencil to draw what you see. (If you want the drawing to be life size, close one eye and use a ruler to measure it. Lightly mark these measurements on your paper.)

4. If you're drawing a flower, try starting from the center before adding the petals. Then add the stems and leaves.

5. Once you've drawn an outline of your plant on the paper, you can begin to add details, shading, and colors as desired to capture the beauty of the herb.

Rose

Rose is my favorite flower to draw. The oldest traces of this flower have been found in Colorado in fossils dating back 35 million years.

Dill

This aromatic herb has delicate, feathery green leaves. It gets its name from the Old English word *dilla*, meaning "to lull." Dill is often used for soothing stomach pain.

BLACKBERRY INK and TWIG PEN

with Molly Meehan Brown

Making inks from plants is as old as human history, with specific practices arising in different cultures. In this activity, you will learn how to make ink using berries and a twig pen for writing and drawing.

MATERIALS

FOR THE BERRY INK

- **2 cups ripe blackberries**
- **Two bowls**
- **Masher or fork**
- **½ cup water**
- **Fine-mesh strainer**
- **Spoon**
- **2 teaspoons white vinegar**
- **2 teaspoons salt**
- **Glass jar with a lid**

FOR THE TWIG PEN

- **Measuring tape or ruler**
- **Clippers**
- **Utility knife**
- **Paper**

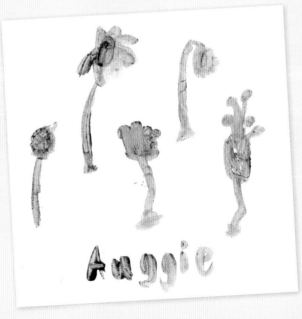

Dip the pen into the blackberry ink to write or draw on the paper.

INSTRUCTIONS

The Berry Ink

1. Place the berries in a bowl and mash them with a masher or fork. Add the water and continue mashing.

2. Set the strainer over the second bowl. Pour in the mashed berries. Press them with the back of the spoon to get as much liquid (ink) as possible.

3. Add the vinegar and salt to the ink, and stir.

4. Pour the ink into your jar and seal with the lid. The ink will be good for up to 2 weeks in the refrigerator.

The Twig Pen

1. Find some green wood, rather than a dead stick that is brittle and dry. With your clippers, cut a twig that is at least 5½ inches long. Remove any leaves.

2. Working with an adult if needed, use a utility knife to trim the end to a fine, chisel-like point, starting about 1 inch from the end. Carve a ½-inch line up from the point to create a channel that will take up the ink.

3. Dip the pen into the blackberry ink to write or draw on the paper.

Vinegar and salt make the ink more vibrant and help it last longer.

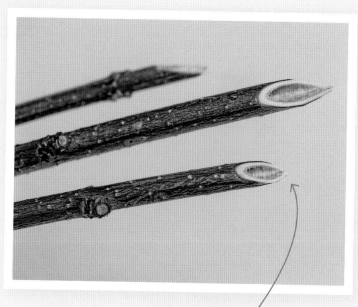

Experiment with cutting different angles on the tip of your twig to see how it changes the width and style of the lines you create.

No-Waste KITCHEN GARDENING

with Arvolyn Hill

Give your food scraps a second life by starting a "regrow" garden—a garden where plants grow from scraps that you might otherwise have thrown away.

MATERIALS

- Scissors
- Scallions
- Basil
- Carrots with greens attached
- Glass jars
- Kitchen knife
- Plate or shallow container
- Pots and potting soil (optional)

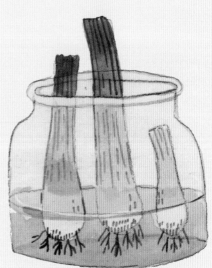

Scallions

Basil

Carrots

INSTRUCTIONS

Scallions

Scallions, also known as green onions, can grow new roots from their white bulbs.

1. Snip the long green stem of each scallion 1 to 2 inches above the white bulb and roots.

2. Stand the scallion bulb-end down in a jar. Add enough room-temperature water to cover the bulb, leaving the trimmed top above the water.

3. Place the jar in a windowsill. After a few days, green shoots will emerge. Change the water once a week.

4. When its shoots are 4 to 5 inches long, plant the scallion in a pot, if desired, or in a garden.

Basil

Basil and many other leafy herbs can be regrown from stem cuttings.

1. Snip off the top 3 to 4 inches from a fresh sprig of basil. Leave the first two sets of leaves at the top (growing end) of the stem, and remove any lower leaves.

2. Place the stem in a jar of water in a warm, sunny spot.

3. Let it sit for a few weeks, until you see that the stem has started to sprout roots.

4. Once the roots are growing well, plant the basil in a pot, if desired, or in a garden.

Carrot Tops

Carrot greens can be regrown from their tops if the leafy greens are still attached.

1. Trim off the top 1 inch of each carrot, leaving the greens intact. (You can trim the greens down to 1 inch if you'd like to eat them.)

2. Place the trimmed tops on a plate or in a shallow container with water.

3. Set the plate or container in a windowsill.

4. In a few days, you will notice roots forming on the carrot stumps and fresh leaves growing on their tops. At this point, plant the carrot tops in a pot, if desired, or in a garden.

NOTE: Planting all regrown plants in a pot with soil is an important step. If you keep them in water, they will be weak and eventually stop growing.

How to SPROUT

with Mason, Amanda, and Amelia Hutchison

Alfalfa sprouts are just about my favorite vegetable to add to salads, sandwiches, wraps, and more. They add freshness and a delightful crunch to whatever you're whipping up in the kitchen.

MATERIALS

- **2 tablespoons alfalfa sprouting seeds, organic if possible**
- **Fine-mesh strainer**
- **Widemouthed quart jar with a canning ring**
- **Sprouting screen**
- **Bowl**

INSTRUCTIONS

1. Pour the seeds into the strainer and rinse them thoroughly with cool water. Remove any debris, stones, or broken seeds.

2. Add the wet seeds to the jar and fill it halfway with slightly warm water. All the seeds should be submerged in the water.

3. Put the sprouting screen on the jar, then screw the canning ring on top. Place the jar in indirect sunlight.

4. Let the seeds soak for at least 8 hours.

5. When the seeds are done soaking, drain the water from the jar.

6. Fill the jar with fresh room-temperature water. Swirl the water around, making sure all the seeds get rinsed. Drain out the water.

Swirl the seeds so they stick to the sides of the jar.

Rinse refrigerated sprouts every 2 to 3 days so they stay moist.

7. Swirl the jar around again to get as many of the seeds to stick to its sides as you can. Place the jar at a 45-degree angle with the screen facing down into the bowl near a window with indirect sunlight. Any remaining water will drain out.

8. Repeat steps 6 and 7 at least once a day for up to 5 days. Germination should begin on the first day, and the sprouts will grow larger and longer with each soaking.

9. Alfalfa sprouts are big enough to eat after 2 to 5 days of growth. Rinse them one final time. Eat them immediately, or cover with a lid and keep in the refrigerator.

Glass Jar
HERB GARDEN

with *Geoffrey Edwards*

As a gardener, I always wonder about what's happening beneath the surface of the soil. When you grow plants in glass jars, you can observe the growth of both the roots and the aerial ("in the air") parts of the plants. You also get to see the small insects, microbes, and mycelia (little white threads of a fungus) at work. It's an entire ecosystem in a jar.

MATERIALS

- Glass jar
- Pebbles or stones
- Potting soil
- Herb seedling of your choosing

NOTE: *I used oregano for my glass jar garden. Basil, chives, mint, parsley, and thyme are also good choices; they are all easy to grow.*

OREGANO is a powerful medicinal herb that is native to the Mediterranean and Asia, though today many different varieties grow abundantly around the globe. Oregano is spicy and delicious and is a favorite in pizza sauce.

INSTRUCTIONS

1. Make sure the jar is clean: Wash it with hot, soapy water; rinse; and then dry.

2. Place small pebbles or stones in the bottom of the jar, about 1 inch deep.

3. Fill the jar about halfway with potting soil. Gently tap it against a table so the soil settles. Add more soil, if needed.

4. Plant the seedling. Add soil until it reaches 2 to 3 inches from the top of glass.

5. Slowly pour room-temperature water into the jar until the water begins to trickle into the pebbles at the bottom.

6. Place the plant in a sunny windowsill. Water whenever the soil is dry and there is no water at the bottom of the jar.

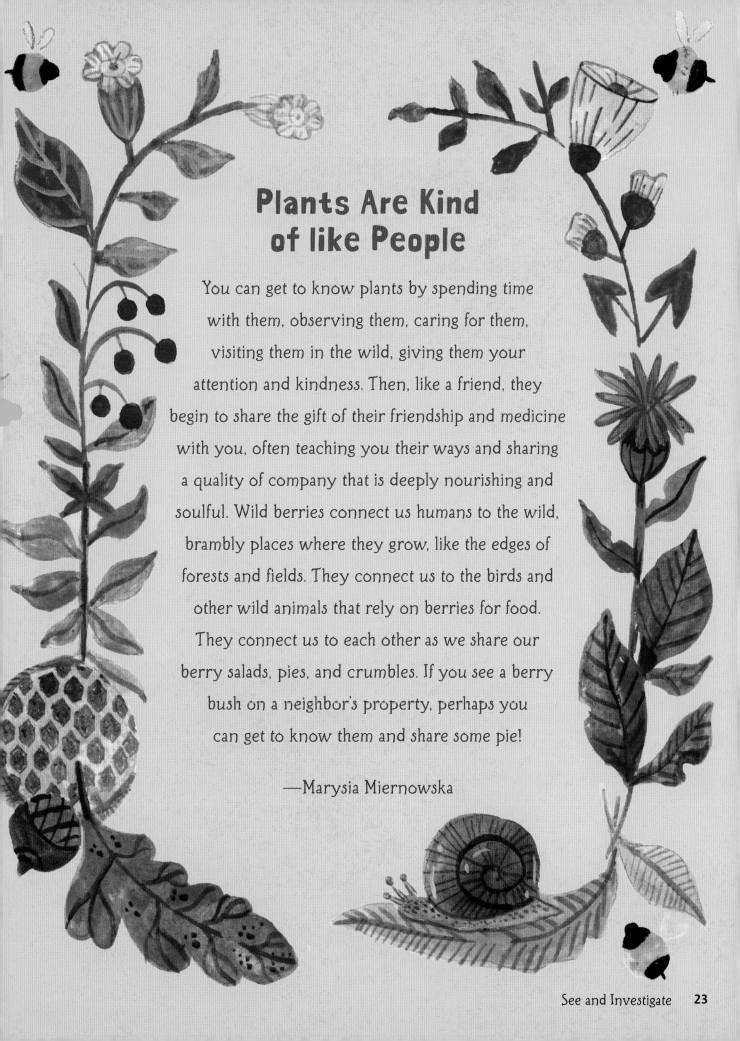

Plants Are Kind of like People

You can get to know plants by spending time with them, observing them, caring for them, visiting them in the wild, giving them your attention and kindness. Then, like a friend, they begin to share the gift of their friendship and medicine with you, often teaching you their ways and sharing a quality of company that is deeply nourishing and soulful. Wild berries connect us humans to the wild, brambly places where they grow, like the edges of forests and fields. They connect us to the birds and other wild animals that rely on berries for food. They connect us to each other as we share our berry salads, pies, and crumbles. If you see a berry bush on a neighbor's property, perhaps you can get to know them and share some pie!

—Marysia Miernowska

Simple ELDERBERRY PROPAGATION

with Kate Backwinkel

An elderberry bush is easy to propagate, or grow from a cutting, and has delicious berries that can be made into jelly, pies, juices, and syrup. Start this project in early spring when the plant is just waking up from its winter sleep. Ask a friend or a neighbor if you can take cuttings from their elderberry, or forage for one with the help of a knowledgeable adult.

MATERIALS

- Clippers
- Bucket
- Pots, for planting
- Potting soil
- 1 tablespoon honey
- Small bowl

nodes

INSTRUCTIONS

1. Using clippers, cut branches from the elderberry bush, each one 6 to 12 inches long with at least two nodes per cutting.

2. Fill the bucket with 1 inch of water. Put the cuttings in the bucket with the cut ends down and soak for 24 hours.

3. Fill your pots with potting soil. You'll need one pot per cutting.

4. Combine the honey with 2 cups of room-temperature water in the bowl and mix well. Dip the end of each cutting into the solution. (Honey boosts root growth and will help your cuttings grow.)

5. Plant each cutting 2 to 3 inches deep in a pot filled with potting soil. Water well.

6. Set the pot indoors near a sunny window or outdoors if weather permits. (The cuttings will not survive a hard frost.) Keep the soil moist. Roots should develop fully in about 3 months. You'll know a cutting is growing well when new leaves emerge.

7. Transplant the plants into the ground. Elderberry likes full sun and moist soil, but it can grow well in partial shade and will become 6 to 12 feet tall. The shrub will produce its sweet-smelling flowers and delicious berries in 2 or 3 years.

New leaves growing on the cutting

The flowers become delicious berries that can be enjoyed by the whole family.

CHAPTER 2

THE TASTE OF NATURE

The kitchen comes alive
With different flavors, smells, and tastes.
I help cut the cilantro and the garlic.
We won't let any go to waste!

A big community celebration,
The dishes infused with herbs,
Cinnamon, hibiscus, rose, and thyme,
The food brings us all together.

At home on a rainy day,
Feeling a chill in the air,
I taste a warm cinnamon tea,
Enjoying a story curled up in my chair.
Each and every herb and spice
Has its unique and special gifts.
Their flavor tells us something
About their medicine.

Using Our Sense of Taste

with Molly Meehan Brown

When I was studying herbalism with my teacher Kat Maier, we began each class with an herbal tea tasting, a tradition we now carry on at Wild Ginger Community Herbal Center. Opening our time together with a cup of tea allows it to be a time to fully arrive, to connect with each other and with the plants.

HERBAL TEA TASTING

1. Make a cup of herbal tea. (Ask an adult for help if you need it.)

2. Sit down with your tea. Breathe in its aroma. How does it smell? Does the smell make you feel awake, relaxed, energized, or something else?

3. Take your first sip of the tea. Notice where you feel the tea in your body. Do you feel it in your belly or in your throat? In your feet or in your hands?

4. Take another sip, and notice the movement of the tea in your body. Does it feel like its warmth and energy are moving upward or downward? Outward or inward?

5. Now, another sip. What does the tea taste like? What is the flavor? Is it sweet, bitter, spicy, sour, or some combination of these flavors?

6. With another sip, ask yourself (if you do not already know) what part of the plant this tea is made from. Is it a root, a bark, a leaf, a seed, or a flower?

7. Last sip. Tune in. Does this tea make you feel warm or cool? Excited or relaxed? Is it moistening (feels like jelly on your tongue) or drying (makes your tongue feel dry or parched)?

Luna's
FAIRY BERRY TEA

with Lupo Passero

Fairies are often closely associated with the edge of the forest, where the elder tree loves to grow. It's said that fairies often live in elder trees, and when the flowers of the trees bend with the wind in the moonlight, it is in fact the fairies riding upon them. Fairies love colorful, tasty, sweet things, which is why we chose elderberries and elderflowers as the main ingredients for this magical tea.

MAKES 9 CUPS

INGREDIENTS

1	tablespoon dried elderberries
1	tablespoon dried elderflowers
½	tablespoon dried hibiscus flowers
½	tablespoon dried rose petals or rosebuds
¼	teaspoon dried spearmint
2–3	cardamom pods, crushed
	Honey or Elderberry Herbal Syrup (page 51), if desired

INSTRUCTIONS

1. Mix the berries, flowers, and herbs together in a bowl with a spoon while singing your favorite song. Fairies love to hear children sing!

2. Bring 1 cup of water to a boil in a pot. (Ask an adult for help if you need it.) Add 1 teaspoon of the berries, flowers, and herbs, cover, and let steep for 10 to 15 minutes.

3. Strain out the berries, flowers, and herbs, then pour the tea into your favorite teacup. Sweeten with honey or Elderberry Herbal Syrup. Store any unused tea blend in a lidded glass jar, out of direct sunlight.

CARDAMOM is one of the world's longest-used spices: It has been grown by humans for more than 4,000 years. It is a very spicy herb and is in the same family as ginger and turmeric. The part of this plant that is most often used is the small, green, oval seed pod, which smells lovely. It is used in curry, rice pudding, and chai tea.

Party
PUNCH

with Aylén Maquehue

When we come together for celebrations, we often share a special beverage. This festive punch looks as magical as it tastes!

SERVES 9–12

INGREDIENTS

9   cups herbal tea, divided

Fruit, berries, edible flowers, citrus peels, and herb leaves

4   cups fruit juice, divided

½   tablespoon turmeric or beet powder

3   cups club soda, kombucha, or ginger beer, for a little fizz (optional)

NOTE: *To make the Botanical Ice Art, you'll need ice cube molds. For our version of this recipe, we used a red tea made with elderflowers, hibiscus flowers, lavender, mint, persimmon leaves, and apple juice.*

INSTRUCTIONS

The Botanical Ice Art

Prepare your ice art at least a day before your event. Make plenty of ice, especially if you're serving the punch on a hot day. A good ratio is 1 part ice to 2 or 3 parts punch.

1. Allow the tea to cool to room temperature.

2. Prepare fruit, berries, flowers, citrus, and herbs by washing, peeling, zesting, slicing, or trimming as necessary.

3. Use 2 cups of the tea and 1 cup of the juice for ice, saving the rest for your punch. Pour a layer of tea into the bottom of a mold, add the botanical elements, and place in the freezer for a few hours. Then pour in a layer of juice, add more botanicals, and freeze.

4. Sprinkle the finished ice with the turmeric and/or beet powder.

The Party Punch

1. Combine the remaining 7 cups tea and 3 cups juice in a punch bowl. Add club soda or another fizzy drink, if desired.

2. Remove your ice art from the molds and add to the punch bowl. (Hold back some of the ice in the freezer to add as needed.)

3. After the party, strain out any leftover plant materials. Thank the plants for sharing their energy with your joyful occasion, and give them back to the earth by composting them.

Use a variety of containers to make ice in interesting shapes.

LAVENDER comes from the Latin word *lavare*, which means "to wash," because of the Roman practice of using it for washing clothes and hair. Its edible and pollinator-friendly flowers are light to dark purple, depending on the variety. Lavender is well known for its distinctive scent, which is calming and relaxing, and it is a popular ingredient in soap, candles, and perfume. One of our favorite ways to use lavender is to infuse it into honey or add it to lemonade.

Fire Cider
OXYMEL

with Molly Meehan Brown

An oxymel is a liquid made with honey and vinegar.
Fire cider contains warming, immune-supportive,
antimicrobial herbs that help clear congestion.
It is often taken in winter throughout the cold
and flu season. We encourage you to create
your own recipe that is full of things you love.

MAKES 4 CUPS

INGREDIENTS

- 2 onions (yellow or red), chopped
- 2 heads garlic, chopped
- 4 tablespoons chopped fresh ginger
- 4 tablespoons chopped horseradish
- 4 tablespoons chopped fresh turmeric
- 1 cayenne, jalapeño, or Scotch bonnet chile pepper, chopped
- 1 lemon, sliced

  Apple cider vinegar

  Honey

INSTRUCTIONS

1. Layer the onions, garlic, ginger, horseradish, turmeric, chile pepper, and lemon in a quart-size jar.

2. Fill the jar three-quarters full with vinegar. Fill the rest of the jar with honey.

3. Seal the jar with its lid. A nonreactive, or nonmetal, lid is best. If your lid is metal, first place a piece of parchment paper on top of the jar; this will keep the metal from corroding. Label your fire cider with the ingredients you used and the date you made it.

4. Let the jar sit on your kitchen counter for 4 to 6 weeks.

5. Strain out the liquid and compost the solids. Keep in the refrigerator or in a cool, dry place.

TO USE: Enjoy ½ to 1 teaspoon for kids and up to 1 tablespoon for adults daily for up to 6 months. If you find the taste too strong, stir the fire cider into a glass of water or juice.

GINGER is one of the most widely used culinary spices on Earth. The rhizome, or root, of this tropical plant is spicy to the taste and can be eaten fresh, cooked, or dried. Ginger is best known for treating nausea.

Spiced Turmeric
KALE CHIPS

with Molly Meehan Brown

Kale chips can be very simple with just a bit of olive oil and salt, or you can be be an herbal explorer and experiment to find new flavors that you love.

SERVES 6

INGREDIENTS

1 bunch fresh kale

¼ cup olive oil (or the oil of your choice)

½ teaspoon salt

¼ teaspoon ground cumin

¼ teaspoon ground ginger

¼ teaspoon turmeric powder

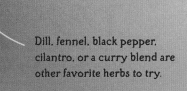

Dill, fennel, black pepper, cilantro, or a curry blend are other favorite herbs to try.

NOTE: *To make kale chips, you'll need a food dehydrator or baking sheets and parchment paper.*

INSTRUCTIONS

1. Remove the kale leaves from the thick stems, then cut or tear the leaves into bite-size pieces. (Ask an adult for help if you need it.) Place in a mixing bowl.

2. Pour the oil over the greens and mix gently.

3. Combine the salt, cumin, ginger, and turmeric in a small bowl. Sprinkle the spice blend over the kale and then toss.

4. Place the kale pieces on dehydrator screens. Dehydrate at 125°F (50°C) until fully crisp, about 5 hours. Check the kale for doneness every 1 to 2 hours.

   Alternatively, preheat your oven to 300°F (150°C). Line baking sheets with parchment paper. Spread the kale over the baking sheets and bake for about 20 minutes, or until crispy.

5. Store any leftovers in an airtight container.

Edible Flower ICE CUBES

with Molly Meehan Brown

Want to impress your friends or family with a fancy garnish for their drink? Or to bring extra botanical joy into your life? Make herbal ice cubes using a variety of edible flowers.

INGREDIENTS

- **Edible herbs and flowers, such as borage, rose, calendula, hibiscus, and lavender**

NOTE: *To make the ice, you'll also need ice cube molds and a tray to set them on.*

INSTRUCTIONS

1. Arrange your ingredients by flavor as well as their visual impact.

2. Place the ice cube molds on a tray to help contain spills when you place them in the freezer.

3. Fill the ice cube molds with the herbs and flowers, then top with water.

4. Freeze for 12 to 24 hours.

HIBISCUS SABDARIFFA, or roselle flower, has bright green and sometimes red edible young leaves with red flower parts around its seed head. These parts are used medicinally. A deep red tea, called sorrel or "rosa de Jamaica," is popular in many countries around the world. Hibiscus is a refrigerant, meaning it cools the body, and is full of vitamin C.

Go on an Herb Walk

One of the best ways to build relationships with the plants that grow around you is to talk to an adult family member about going on an herb walk with a local expert. Not only will you learn about all of the amazing plants in your area, but you will also get to meet other folks who are interested in nature, including the teacher and the other people on the herb walk.

Plant people are the best!

Garden-Fresh LUNCH

with Molly Meehan Brown

Throughout the growing season, healthy, delicious meals can be made straight from the garden or farmers' market. The best meals are cooked with love and gratitude. Ask an adult for help with preparing the recipes if you need it.

SERVES 4–6

Berry and Greens Salad

INGREDIENTS

3   cups salad greens
1   cucumber
1   cup raspberries
½   cup olive oil
¼   cup apple cider vinegar
¼   cup honey

INSTRUCTIONS

1. Roughly chop the salad greens and transfer to a serving bowl.

2. Slice the cucumber and spread it on top of the greens. Top with the berries.

3. Make a simple salad dressing by whisking together the oil, vinegar, and honey. Pour the dressing over the salad and toss before serving.

Zucchini Fritters

INGREDIENTS

1   zucchini
    Salt
1   cup cornmeal
1   egg
1   tablespoon chopped fresh dill or cilantro
    Freshly ground black pepper
1   tablespoon olive oil

INSTRUCTIONS

1. Cut off the ends of the zucchini. Use a grater to grate the zucchini into a bowl. Add a pinch of salt to the grated zucchini and toss well.

2. Set a strainer over your sink or a large bowl. Transfer the grated zucchini to the strainer and let drain for 15 to 20 minutes.

3. Put the drained zucchini in a large bowl. Add the cornmeal, egg, and dill or cilantro. Season generously with salt and pepper. Mix well.

4. Heat the oil in a skillet over medium heat. Working in batches, drop heaping tablespoons of batter into the skillet. Flatten slightly with the back end of a spoon or spatula. Cook fritters evenly on both sides until lightly browned, 3 to 5 minutes on each side.

5. Set the fritters on paper towels to soak up any excess oil before serving.

Vegetable Frittata

INGREDIENTS

8   eggs
¼   cup milk or cream
½   teaspoon salt
½   teaspoon freshly ground black pepper
1   cup chopped kale
1   cup chopped green bell pepper
½   cup chopped onion
2   garlic cloves, chopped

INSTRUCTIONS

1. Preheat the oven to 375°F (190°C).

2. Crack the eggs into a bowl. Add the milk or cream and whisk well. Add the salt and black pepper and whisk again.

3. Place the vegetables in a 9-inch round or square baking dish. Pour the egg mixture over them.

4. Bake for 35 to 45 minutes, or until a knife inserted in the center comes out clean.

Decorative HERBAL PIZZAS

with Molly Meehan Brown

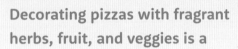

Decorating pizzas with fragrant herbs, fruit, and veggies is a great way to have fun and be creative in the kitchen. Use your toppings to create a scene, such as a sunny day with flowers, or an abstract pattern.

SERVES 4

INGREDIENTS

Oil, for greasing the pan

Pizza dough, homemade or store-bought

½ cup sauce: tomato, creamy Alfredo, or pesto (see facing page)

½ cup shredded dairy or plant-based cheese (optional)

Vegetables, fruit, and herbs for toppings: peppers, onions, shiso, spinach, tomatoes, figs, basil, fennel, oregano, rosemary, thyme, or tulsi

INSTRUCTIONS

1. Preheat your oven to 400°F (200°C). Oil a baking pan or use a pizza stone.

2. Stretch the dough over your pan or pizza stone.

3. Lightly spread the sauce over the dough, using a ladle or spoon. Sprinkle the cheese, if you're using it, on top.

4. Arrange your toppings on the pizza, trimming them as needed to create the shapes and designs you want.

5. Bake for 12 to 15 minutes. (Ask an adult for help putting the pizza in the oven and taking it out, if you need it.)

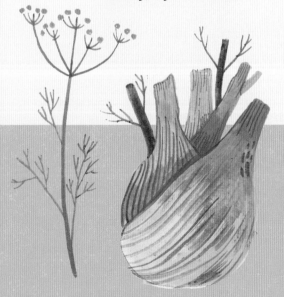

FENNEL is a lovely plant that can grow very tall, with large, sturdy bulbs at the bottom, hollow stems shooting toward the sky, and bright yellow flowers that look like fireworks at the top. Every part of the plant can be used—root, stems, flowers, and seeds. The seeds, which taste like black licorice, are made into a delicious tea that supports digestion, and you can roast the bulb and eat it whole.

CHICKWEED PESTO

with Molly Meehan Brown

This recipe changes depending on what plants are growing. In spring, we use foraged chickweed. Later in the season, we use spinach, kale, or shiso.

MAKES 2½ CUPS

INGREDIENTS

- 3 cups fresh herbs (chickweed, basil, cilantro, or any of the leafy greens mentioned above)
- 1 cup pine nuts, cashews, walnuts, or sunflower seeds
- 1 garlic clove, crushed
- Juice of 1 lemon
- 1 cup olive oil
- Salt and freshly ground black pepper

NOTE: *To make pesto, you'll need a food processor or blender. If using a blender, in step 2, you may want to add the oil at the same time as you add the herbs, nuts, garlic, and lemon juice, for smoother blending.*

INSTRUCTIONS

1. Combine the herbs, nuts, garlic, and lemon juice in a food processor or blender (see note). Blend until the leaves are all chopped up. (Ask an adult for help if you need it.)

2. If using a food processor, with the motor running, slowly pour the oil into the food processor through its feed chute. Turn off the motor, scrape the sides with a spatula, and taste. Add salt and pepper to taste. Process until smooth.

CHICKWEED is a wild plant that is found primarily in North America and Europe. It has many culinary and folk remedy uses that date back for centuries. Birds, rabbits, deer, and even people eat chickweed. It can be made into a tea, and it makes a delicious and nutritious foraged green. In warm climates, chickweed grows rapidly and abundantly in early spring and reappears again when temperatures cool in fall.

Rundown STEW

with Alda Cook Campbell

Rundown is a stew made in the small fishing village where I live in the Caribe Sur of Costa Rica. My ancestors brought this dish with them from Jamaica. When I was a little girl, my grandmother, whom everybody called Miss Edith, would send us to go "run down" the fresh vegetables and roots from the garden and the fresh-caught fish and seafood from the day. While this stew traditionally uses seafood such as fish, lobster, and crab, we have adapted this recipe to use plants.

Traditionally, rundown was made over an open fire.

SERVES 8

INGREDIENTS

- 4 (13.5-ounce) cans coconut milk
- 3 cups chopped yuca, nami, or sweet potato
- 1 cup chopped green banana or plantain
- ½ cup chopped carrot
- 1 bell pepper, chopped
- 1 onion, chopped
- 4 large garlic cloves, chopped
- ½ teaspoon fresh thyme or ¼ teaspoon dried
- ½ teaspoon salt
- ½ teaspoon freshly ground black pepper
- 1 Panamanian or Scotch bonnet chile pepper

INSTRUCTIONS

1. Combine the coconut milk with 6 cups water in a large pot. Add the yuca, green banana, carrot, bell pepper, onion, garlic, thyme, salt, and black pepper. Bring to a boil, then reduce the heat to keep the stew at a simmer. (Ask an adult for help if you need it.)

2. Add the chile pepper. Let the stew simmer for 30 to 40 minutes. Remove the chile before serving.

THYME has deep green, oval, almost-glossy leaves and tiny light purple flowers. It is a very common kitchen herb and is used medicinally to treat colds, coughs, and sore throats.

Herbalism and Lineage

Each one of us has a lineage that includes people who have worked with plants. Our lineage can include our ancestors and the communities we come from as well as the people we have learned from.

Over time and for many reasons, many of us have been separated from the relationships and practices of our ancestors. That's not true for all of us; many communities have held on to their practices, and many have done so quietly in order to protect them. But each of our ancestral herbal lineages are ours to claim, and the plants themselves can be our teachers in how to live and to be in service to our community.

I invite you to explore your own lineage and reconnect with the wisdom and practices that your ancestors made use of. By relearning and reclaiming the plant practices of your lineage, you can help make up for what has been lost and plant seeds for the future.

EXPLORE YOUR LINEAGE

- What lineage/s are you a part of?

- What were the practices and rituals your ancestors held around herbs?

- Who practiced herbalism and in what way?

- How does this shape your path as a plant person?

Hot Summer Day ICE POPS

with Molly Meehan Brown

Ice pops are a delicious way to enjoy your favorite herbs and stay cool on a hot day.

INGREDIENTS

Fresh or dried herbs for the base flavor (try bee balm, catnip, chamomile, lemon balm, mint, or thyme)

Sugar, maple syrup, herbal syrup, or other sweetener of your choice

Fresh herbs and edible flowers for decoration (try dill, fennel, lavender, or passionflower)

NOTE: *To make the ice pops, you'll need silicone pop molds or plastic cups and craft sticks.*

INSTRUCTIONS

1. Measure out enough water to fill your molds or cups. Add 2 tablespoons of fresh herbs or 1 teaspoon of dried herbs for every 1 cup of water.

2. Bring the water to a boil in a pot. (Ask an adult for help if you need it.) Add the herbs, cover, and let steep for 10 to 15 minutes off the heat.

3. Strain out the herbs. Add sweetener to taste and stir to dissolve. Then let the tea cool completely.

4. Arrange the decorative herbs and flowers in the molds or cups. Then fill the molds or cups with the tea.

5. Place in your freezer. After 40 minutes or so, when the pops are slushy, insert the sticks. Allow to fully freeze. Carefully remove the pops from the molds and enjoy!

BEE BALM, also known as monarda, wild oregano, or bergamot, grows naturally in North America. Bee balm provides food and habitat for hummingbirds, butterflies, honeybees, and more. Rubbing its leaves on skin helps relieve the pain of bee stings, which is where this plant got its name.

Pistachio–Goji Berry CHOCOLATE

with Mason, Amanda, and Amelia Hutchison

For the longest time, I thought making chocolate was best left to the professionals. Eventually my curiosity got the best of me, and I researched how to make chocolate at home. Much to my delight, there is an incredibly easy way, which is the recipe I am sharing with you here. Chocolate and its lineage are rooted in the Indigenous communities of Central and South America, and I encourage you to honor and explore these origins.

MAKES 3½ CUPS

INGREDIENTS

- 1 cup roasted cocoa butter wafers
- 1 cup roasted cacao powder
- ½ cup maple syrup
- ½ cup crunchy peanut butter
- ¼ cup goji berries, divided
- ¼ cup chopped pistachios

Cut the chocolate into pieces after it cools.

INSTRUCTIONS

1. Put the cocoa butter wafers in a saucepan. Warm over medium heat until they melt. (Ask an adult for help if you need it.)

2. Pour in the cacao powder and whisk until it's combined with the wafers. Then remove the pan from the heat and let cool for 10 minutes.

3. Add the maple syrup, peanut butter, and half of the goji berries. Stir until fully combined.

4. Line a sheet pan with parchment paper. Pour the chocolate onto the parchment and use a spatula to spread it across the pan until it is smooth and even.

5. Sprinkle the remaining goji berries on top, then transfer the pan to your freezer to cool for 30 minutes before serving. Sprinkle the pistachios on top before serving.

COCONUT DROPS

with Zenovia D'Arienzo

Trinidad and Tobago is a two-island nation in the Caribbean near Venezuela. It is home to diverse people, and the food is a fusion of all the cultures found there. Coconut Drops are a shortbread delight. I loved them as a child and love making them with my children. They remind me of my childhood and home on the islands of sweet T&T.

MAKES 14–16 DROPS

INGREDIENTS

- 2 teaspoons ground cinnamon
- ⅛ teaspoon ground nutmeg
- 1 tablespoon coconut milk
- 1 cup all-purpose flour
- 1 teaspoon baking powder
- 4 tablespoons unsalted butter, at room temperature
- 1 cup granulated sugar, divided
- 1 egg
- 2 teaspoons vanilla extract
- ½ teaspoon grated lemon zest
- 2 cups fresh or frozen grated unsweetened coconut
- Light brown sugar crystals, for sprinkling on top

INSTRUCTIONS

1. Preheat the oven to 400°F (200°C). Line a baking sheet with parchment paper. (Ask an adult for help if you need it.)

2. Combine the cinnamon, nutmeg, and coconut milk in a small bowl. Mix well, then set aside.

3. Sift the flour and baking powder together into a bowl.

4. In a separate bowl, combine the butter and ½ cup of the granulated sugar. Using a hand mixer on high speed, mix until creamy and fluffy, about 4 minutes. Add the egg and vanilla, and beat for 2 minutes.

5. Fold the lemon zest, coconut milk–spice mixture, and grated coconut into the batter by hand.

6. Using a tablespoon, drop spoonfuls of the batter onto the prepared baking sheet, keeping them 1 inch apart.

7. Bake for 15 minutes, or until golden brown. Let cool on a wire rack.

8. While the coconut drops are cooling, make a glaze: Combine the remaining ½ cup granulated sugar with ¾ cup water in a saucepan. Stir until the sugar completely dissolves in the water, then bring to a simmer. Continue stirring until it thickens and turns an almost amber color, then remove from the heat.

9. Brush the glaze onto the cooled drops. Sprinkle the brown sugar crystals on top, then serve.

NUTMEG is a spice made by grinding the seed of the fruit from a nutmeg tree into a powder. You must live somewhere sunny and hot and be very patient to grow a nutmeg tree. It takes up to 4 years for it to produce flowers and up to 15 years to produce fruit. Nutmeg is used in foods such as garam masala from India, tortellini from Italy, and traditional American holiday treats like pumpkin pie and eggnog.

CINNAMON has been used as a spice for thousands of years, dating back to ancient Egypt. It is made from the inner bark of the cinnamon tree, which is harvested and then dried into rolls called cinnamon sticks. The sticks can be ground to form powder. Cinnamon is commonly found in apple pie and cinnamon buns or made into a tea. It is also germ-fighting, making it a popular addition to toothpaste.

Wild Berry
CRUMBLE

with Marysia and Flora Miernowska and Ira Christian

One of the great joys of late summer is picking luscious, ripe blackberries off the vine in the warm sun from your local fields or wild spaces. Store-bought blackberries can be used in this recipe as well.

SERVES 6–8

INGREDIENTS

FOR THE FILLING
- ½ cup fresh elderberries or ⅓ cup dried
- 4½ cups blackberries
- ⅓ cup coconut sugar (or other sweetener of your choice)
- ¼ cup flour (oat, wheat, or other flour of your choice)
- Juice of ½ lemon (1–2 tablespoons)

FOR THE TOPPING
- 1½ cups rolled oats
- ¾ cup finely chopped almonds
- ½ teaspoon ground cinnamon
- ¼ teaspoon salt
- 4 tablespoons butter, chopped into small cubes

FOR THE WHIPPED CREAM
- 1 cup whipping cream
- ¼ teaspoon vanilla extract
- 1 tablespoon maple syrup or ½ teaspoon sugar of your choice (optional)

INSTRUCTIONS

The Filling

1. Preheat the oven to 375°F (190°C). (Ask an adult for help if you need it.)

2. If you are using dried elderberries, put them in a bowl and pour ⅓ cup boiling water over them. Let sit for 10 minutes, stir, and let sit for another 10 minutes. The berries should absorb most of the water as they rehydrate.

3. Mix the elderberries (fresh or rehydrated) with the blackberries, sugar, flour, and lemon juice in a medium bowl. Pour directly into a 9-inch round or square pan.

The Topping

1. Mix the oats, almonds, cinnamon, and salt together in a large bowl. Add the butter, and use a spoon or your fingers to spread the butter evenly throughout the mixture. Sprinkle the topping evenly over the berry filling.

2. Bake for 30 to 40 minutes. Let cool for 20 minutes to 1 hour.

The Whipped Cream

1. Combine the cream, vanilla, and maple syrup or other sweetener, if using, in a jar or other container that can be sealed. Seal, then shake for 5 to 10 minutes, until the cream is fully whipped.

2. Serve the crumble in bowls, adding a dollop of whipped cream on top.

ELDER shrubs can be found throughout the world and are easy to identify by their leaves, which are arranged in opposite pairs with five to seven long, serrated (tooth-edged) leaves on each stem. In spring, the bush blooms with tiny cream-colored or white flowers that smell sweet and can be used for tea or sprinkled on desserts. In late summer, the pollinated flowers become elderberries. These wild berries are a powerful medicinal food. They feed birds and other wildlife and humans, but they are only safe to eat if they are cooked or dried. Elderberries boost your immunity, helping you fight off colds. They are high in vitamin C and antioxidants and have antiviral properties.

CHAPTER 3

SWEET AND SPICY SMELLS

Smell can bring us back in time,
Bring a memory alive,
Like your grandma's apple cinnamon pie,
Or herb-infused honey from your local beehive.
The scent of lavender helps bring peace and calm,
While rosemary helps us remember.
Peppermint helps us focus,
And chamomile helps us rest and stay calm in our center.

On a summer afternoon,
When my neighbors cut their pasture,
The scent of sweet grass fills the air,
Lulling me with its sweet allure.

Take a moment to breathe in and out,
To simply be with each plant.
Connect with how they make you feel
When you notice their special scent.

Rosemary Water
MiST

with Landis Pulido

Here is an invitation to connect with your sense of smell and build a relationship with the aromatic herb rosemary, or romero, as it is known in Spanish. This plant invites calming, grounding energy. Water and heat bring out the beautiful medicine and create a sacred mist for you, your home, and your family.

MAKES 4 CUPS

MATERIALS

- Pot
- Five rosemary branches, each about 5 inches long
- Funnel
- 32-ounce glass spray bottle
- Ladle
- Strainer
- Marker and masking tape, for labeling

ROSEMARY is native to North Africa, Asia, and Europe and thrives in warm climates. Its distinctive scent is captivating. "Rosemary is for remembrance" is a common phrase you'll hear in the herbal community, as this plant has long been used to support memory.

INSTRUCTIONS

1. Fill a pot with 4 cups of water. Add the rosemary branches. Place the pot on your stove and bring the water to a boil. (Ask an adult for help if you need it.)

2. Turn off the heat and cover the pot with a lid. Leave the rosemary steeping for 1 hour, or until the water in the pot cools to room temperature.

3. Place the funnel into your spray bottle. Using a ladle, pour the rosemary-infused water through the strainer and into the funnel to fill the spray bottle. Pour slowly, and enjoy the smell of the rosemary.

4. Write "Rosemary Water Mist" and the date on the masking tape. Apply the tape as a label to the spray bottle. Store the mist in your refrigerator for up to 2 weeks. Spray it into the air whenever you want a room freshener.

Elderberry
HERBAL SYRUP

with Molly Meehan Brown

Elderberries grow abundantly where we live, with their lovely, sweet-smelling white flowers in spring and then deep purple fruit ripening in July. While you can make a syrup with just elderberries, we love to add hibiscus and rose hips, which are high in vitamin C and have a delicious sour flavor, plus cinnamon and a little bit of cardamom to add warmth along with their own healing benefits.

MAKES 4 CUPS

INGREDIENTS

- 1 cup fresh or dried elderberries
- ½ cup hibiscus flowers
- ½ cup rose hips
- ¼ cup ground cinnamon
- ½ teaspoon ground cardamom
- 2 cups honey

INSTRUCTIONS

1. Fill a pot with 4 cups of water. Add the elderberries, hibiscus, rose hips, cinnamon, and cardamom. Place the pot on your stove and bring to a simmer. (Ask an adult for help if you need it.) Let simmer until the water is reduced by half, 10 to 15 minutes.

2. Strain out and compost the herbs. Add the honey and slowly stir with a spoon. Let the herb-infused water cool.

3. When it's ready, pour your elderberry syrup into a jar. Store in the refrigerator, where it will keep for 2 weeks.

TO USE: Enjoy a teaspoon of syrup once a day, or up to four times a day when you need extra immune support.

Tummy Trouble TEA

with Angela Rahim

Lemon balm smells like lemon with a hint of mint. It gives this tea a lemony flavor and helps soothe our bellies. The nettle leaves also help nourish us when we are not feeling the best.

MAKES 5 CUPS

INGREDIENTS

- 3 **teaspoons dried lemon balm**
- 2 **teaspoons dried nettle leaf**
- 1 **teaspoon honey (optional)**

INSTRUCTIONS

1. Stir together the lemon balm and nettle leaf in a small bowl.

2. Boil 1 cup of water in a teakettle. (Ask an adult for help if you need it.)

3. Place 1 teaspoon of the herbs in a teacup. Pour the boiling water over the herbs. Cover and let steep for 5 minutes.

4. Strain out the herbs. Stir in the honey, if desired. Enjoy. Store the remaining dried tea mix in a jar with a lid.

NETTLE, or stinging nettle, is a wild plant full of nourishing minerals that tastes like spinach when cooked. Its leaves and stems are very bright green, with white or light green flowers and seeds that eventually turn black. For food or tea, the young tops of the plant are best. Nettle stings until cooked or dried, so wear gloves when handling. Nettle tea tastes very earthy and has a beautiful deep green color.

Plants Teach Us

One amazing thing about plants is they can
teach us what they are helpful for.
When we look carefully, we can observe
certain clues about a plant's uses.

For example, many people find the scent of
lavender to be very relaxing, and the flowers are a
soothing, soft shade between violet and blue. A walnut
is shaped like a brain, and a walnut contains essential
fatty acids that nourish our brain health! Many herbs
that help protect and strengthen our heart, such as
hawthorn, hibiscus, and rose hips, are red, just like
the blood flowing through our cardiovascular system!
Herbalists call this the "doctrine of signatures."

How a plant makes you feel when you smell it, its
shape or color, the patterns on its leaves, and even
where it grows can potentially tell you something
about the plant's helpful properties. You can
make a practice of using your senses with
each new plant you meet.

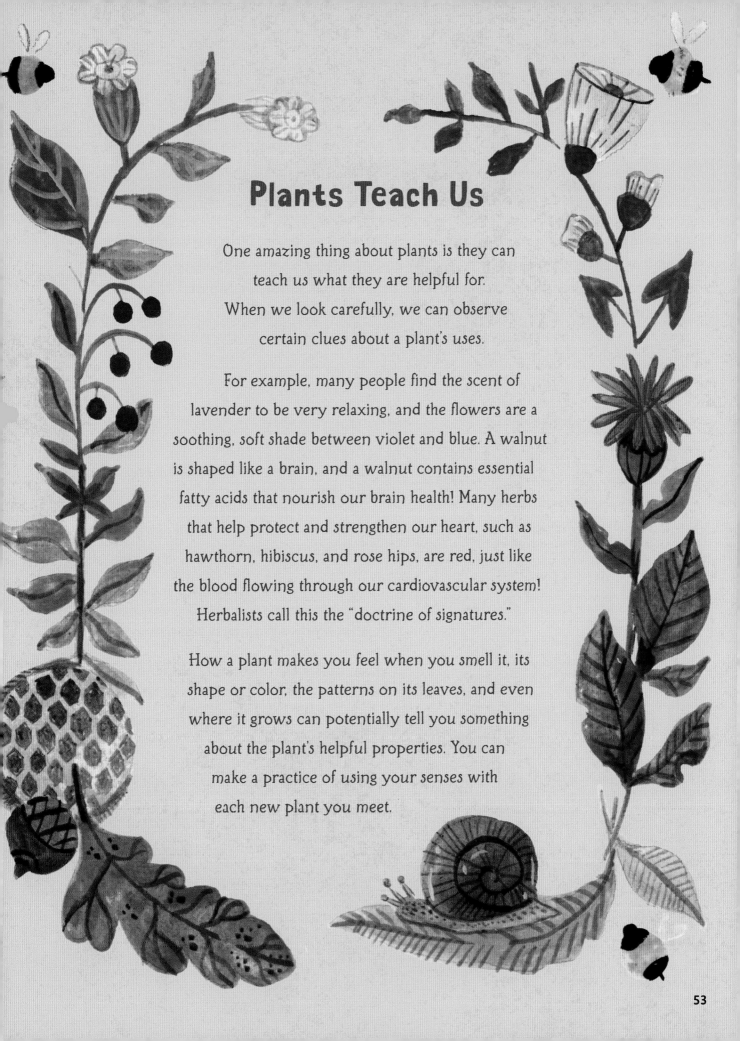

Herb and Spice
APPLE-PEAR TOPPING

with Molly Meehan Brown

There is something so deeply nourishing about fruit baked with the warm and spicy scents of cinnamon, ginger, and nutmeg. Use this topping on pancakes and oatmeal, in muffins and other baked goods, on top of yogurt, as a basic pie filling, and even as an afternoon snack.

MAKES 1½ CUPS

INGREDIENTS

- 2 apples
- 2 pears
- ½ teaspoon ground cinnamon
- ½ teaspoon ground ginger
- ¼ teaspoon ground nutmeg

INSTRUCTIONS

1. Preheat your oven to 375°F (190°C). (Ask an adult for help if you need it.)

2. Slice the apples and pears, then place the sliced fruit in a small baking dish.

3. Combine the cinnamon, ginger, and nutmeg in a bowl and mix well. Sprinkle the spice mix evenly over the apples and pears.

4. Bake for 15 to 20 minutes, or until the fruit has warmed and softened to your liking.

Kitchen
WREATH

with Molly Meehan Brown

Create a summertime herbal wreath with classic herbs known for their special scents. The wreath makes a pretty decoration, and the herbs can also be used for cooking, even after the leaves dry out.

MATERIALS

- Lavender, rosemary, sage, thyme, or bay stems
- Floral wire (found in craft stores)
- Clippers or wire cutters
- Wreath frame (handmade or purchased)

INSTRUCTIONS

1. Gather each set of herbs in small bunches approximately 4 to 8 inches long. Strip the leaves from the bottom of each bunch, and wrap the stems together tightly with wire. Leave extra wire to attach the herbs to the frame.

2. Attach the first bunch of herbs to the wreath frame, securing it with the wire. Layer the next bunch on top of the first, overlapping it just enough to hide the wire.

3. Continue to add herb bunches to the frame. Every so often, step back and hold up your wreath to see if it looks full and balanced.

4. When you get to your last bunch, lift the first bunch and tuck the ends of the last bunch underneath.

5. Hang the finished wreath in your kitchen, or give it to a friend who loves to cook.

Lemon Balm
LiP BALM

with Molly Meehan Brown

Lip balms are fun and easy to make, with endless variations. One of my favorites is made with lemon balm, which adds a yummy and uplifting lemony scent. Feel free to try other herbs, such as anise, cinnamon, or peppermint.

MAKES 16 OUNCES

INGREDIENTS

½ cup dried lemon balm or 1 cup fresh

1 cup oil (almond, apricot, sunflower, or olive)

½ cup beeswax or beeswax pastilles

½ cup cocoa butter

NOTE: *You'll need metal or heatproof glass containers for storing the balm. I like to use little tins (½ to 1 ounce) so I can carry my lip balm with me.*

INSTRUCTIONS

1. If you are using fresh lemon balm, leave it out at room temperature overnight to wilt (see page 92).

2. Set up a double boiler with water in the bottom pan. (Ask an adult for help if you need it.) In the top pan, add the oil and lemon balm. Set over very low heat for approximately 5 hours, checking frequently and adding water as needed. (Never allow the oil to heat to the point of bubbling.)

3. After the lemon balm has infused into the oil, strain out the herbs, composting them if possible.

4. Combine the infused oil, beeswax, and cocoa butter in a pan that is used only for beeswax preparations; you won't want to cook food in it afterward. Warm over very low heat until all the ingredients have melted together. Stir well.

5. Pour the mixture into metal or glass containers. Cool until hardened. Lip balm will keep for up to 6 months. Avoid high temperatures to prevent melting.

Evergreen SALVE

with Molly Meehan Brown

A salve is used to soothe and heal our skin. This recipe calls for pine and thyme, plants that smell nice, with an aroma that reminds us of winter and the end-of-year holiday season.

MAKES 10 OUNCES

INGREDIENTS

- ½ cup fresh pine needles
- ½ cup fresh thyme (if harvesting, cut 3-inch sprigs to avoid damaging the plant)
- 1 cup oil (sunflower, olive, coconut, shea, jojoba, or almond)
- ¼ cup beeswax or beeswax pastilles
- 2 drops pine essential oil (optional)
- 2 drops thyme essential oil (optional)

NOTE: *You'll need metal or heatproof glass containers for storing the salve.*

PINE is one of my all-time favorite scents—it's super refreshing and spicy. In the region of North America where I live, the eastern white pine is one of my most beloved native trees. It is an evergreen, meaning it does not drop its leaves (its needles), during winter.

INSTRUCTIONS

1. Chop the pine needles and thyme. (Ask an adult for help if you need it.)

2. Set up a double boiler with water in the bottom pan. In the top pan, add the oil, pine, and thyme. Set over very low heat for approximately 1 to 3 hours, checking frequently and adding water as needed. (Never allow the oil to get so hot that it bubbles.)

3. After the needles and herbs have infused into the oil, strain out the plant material, composting it if possible.

4. Place the beeswax in a pan that is used only for beeswax preparations; you won't want to cook food in it afterward. Add ¾ cup of the infused oil. Warm over very low heat until the beeswax melts completely.

5. Stir in the pine and/or thyme essential oil, if using, and pour the mixture into metal or glass storage containers. Attach the lids immediately. Let cool until hardened. This salve will last indefinitely. Just be sure to use clean, dry hands when taking a scoop!

Peppermint GLYCERITE

with Molly Meehan Brown

A glycerite is a mild, sweet herbal medicine made from an extract of herbs in vegetable glycerin. Peppermint glycerite uplifts the spirit whenever you smell its sharp, cool, and refreshing scent, and it can make your stomach feel better when it's upset. Try adding it to hot chocolate for a minty delight!

MAKES 1 CUP

INGREDIENTS

1   cup chopped fresh peppermint or ¼ cup dried
1   cup vegetable glycerin

> **NOTE:** *To make the glycerite, you'll need a heatproof mason jar with a lid. To store it, use dropper bottles—small, dark glass bottles with an eyedropper lid.*

INSTRUCTIONS

1. Fill a heatproof glass jar with the peppermint and glycerin and close the lid on top.

2. Fill a pot with about 3 inches of water and heat until simmering. (Ask an adult for help if you need it.) Place the filled jar in the water and simmer for 30 minutes.

3. Using a hot pad or tongs, carefully take the jar out of the water and place it on a heatproof surface. Do not place the jar on a cold surface, as the sudden change in temperature can cause it to shatter. Let cool.

4. Once the jar has cooled to room temperature, strain out and compost the peppermint. Pour the glycerite into glass bottles or jars with lids for storage.

5. Store the glycerite out of direct sunlight, in a place where temperatures don't get higher than 95°F (35°C) or below 32°F (0°C). It will keep for 1 year.

TO USE: Take 3 to 5 drops two or three times a day.

How to Label

Labeling your herb-infused teas, oils, salves, syrups, and other remedies is essential. You can write your label on paper and tape it on your jar, or you can use tape itself as a label. You could also buy blank labels or even print custom labels!

WHAT TO INCLUDE ON YOUR LABEL:

- Common name of each plant you used
- Latin names of the plants
- Plant parts used
- Whether the plants were fresh or dried
- Other ingredients
- Date prepared

Peppermint Glycerite
Peppermint (*Mentha piperita*)
Fresh leaves
Vegetable glycerin
12/12/24

PEPPERMINT offers the minty flavor we enjoy in candy canes, mint chocolate chip ice cream, and toothpaste. Peppermint tea, made from the fresh or dried leaves of the plant, has helped ease stomachaches for thousands of years. This perennial (meaning it comes back every year) plant is easily identified by its fresh, clean scent and its hot-then-cool taste. Peppermint and other members of the mint family can be found in gardens, grocery stores, or garden centers, or you can easily grow it from seed. But watch out: When planted, this herb loves to spread. Instead of planting it right in the ground, you might want to plant it in a pot to keep it in one place.

CHAPTER 4

LET'S USE OUR HANDS

Plants help bring our senses alive.
Some are smooth and some are textured.
Some have little hairs or thorns,
Some help soothe and some are a mixture.

Feeling a tickle in my throat,
Maybe red and sore and achy,
I gather marshmallow root for a soak in water,
And its slippery mucilage helps immediately.

Feeling the leaves of mullein,
They are smooth and soft and look like wool.
While aloe vera looks like jelly,
Inside its leaves, it feels cool.

Stinging nettles are deep green
And nourishing and helpful.
But their leaves and stems sting when touched,
So when harvesting, we must be careful.

NATURAL DYE
with Turmeric

with *sumi dutta*

Get your shine on (and your hands a little stained) with this gorgeous turmeric dye project. Turn white T-shirts, pillowcases, bandanas, tote bags, and more into a burst of sunshine.

MATERIALS

- White 100% cotton fabric item
- Large bowl
- Large stainless steel pot (5 quarts, or a size large enough to fit your fabric when the pot is two-thirds full of water)
- Tablespoon
- Small bowl

- ⅓ cup turmeric powder
- Rubber bands or string, for tie-dyeing (optional)
- Tongs
- Large wooden spoon

NOTE TO PARENTS: *Turmeric will stain (that's what makes it a good dye!), so use rubber gloves and aprons, and consider taking the whole activity outdoors.*

INSTRUCTIONS

Prepare Your Fabric

1. Prewash the item you're going to dye in warm, soapy water to remove any dirt or chemicals that would prevent the turmeric from dyeing the fabric evenly.

2. Soak the fabric in cold water in a large bowl while you move on to the next steps.

Make the Paste

1. Fill the pot two-thirds full with water and place it on a stove.

2. Measure 2 tablespoons of water into the small bowl. Add the turmeric, 1 tablespoon at a time, stirring well, to make a bright yellow paste.

3. Add the paste to the water in the pot and stir until it dissolves. Bring the water to a simmer over medium heat.

4. While the water heats up, remove the item you'll be dyeing from the water it's been soaking in. Squeeze out any excess water. (See page 64 for tie-dye instructions.)

Dye Your Fabric

1. Use the tongs to slowly add your fabric to the pot.

2. Push the item down with the wooden spoon to submerge it, and stir. All of the fabric should be fully covered with dye.

3. Simmer for at least 30 minutes. (The longer you leave it, the darker the color will be.) Turn off the heat when you are happy with the shade.

4. Using the tongs, slowly remove your item from the dye pot. (If you tied it up, unfold it.) Thoroughly rinse the fabric with cold water. Check to make sure there's no turmeric powder on the cloth!

continued on page 64

Make a paste from the turmeric and water.

The dye is simmering when you see tiny bubbles.

The folds and ties act as a resist, preventing the dye from coloring the fabric.

5. Squeeze any remaining water out of your item. Hang it in a shady spot to dry. (Direct sun will fade the color.)

NOTE: Make sure to hand-wash and line-dry your dyed item, as the color is likely to run and stain other fabrics. The color will also fade with washing. You can always re-dye the fabric to keep it fresh and vibrant!

How to Tie-Dye

Fold your fabric into a small triangle or square and tie it up so that it looks like a little cloth dumpling, or section off several small portions of the cloth, using string or rubber bands to secure them.

Unique and colorful, tie-dyed fabrics always look great!

TURMERIC has gorgeous deep green leaves, but the bright orange rhizome (underground stem), with its thin, almost stringlike roots, is the real star of the show. Turmeric has lots of health benefits for your body and your brain. Because it fights inflammation and supports the digestive system, it has a wide variety of uses, whether taken internally (by drinking or eating) or used topically (applied to skin). Turmeric is traditionally used in making Indian curry and gives it its yellow color. At the grocery store, you can find turmeric powder in the spice aisle or fresh turmeric in the produce section.

Fresh Herb
CARDS AND INVITATIONS

with Molly Meehan Brown

There is nothing quite like receiving a handwritten birthday card, thank-you note, or invitation to a special celebration. Adding freshly picked herbs to the envelope adds to the joy.

MATERIALS

- Card and envelope
- Pen
- Clipping(s) of your favorite herb or flower
- Natural string or yarn
- Protective envelope (if mailing)

INSTRUCTIONS

1. Write your greeting or message in the card and put it in an envelope.

2. Tie clippings to the outside of the envelope using the string or yarn. Secure tightly with a bow or knot.

3. Write the name of the herb or flower so the receiver knows the name of your special plant friend.

4. Enclose the card in a protective envelope to send in the mail, or give it directly to your friend or loved one.

Borage + Rosemary

Pressed Flower
COLLAGE

with Toni Roberts

Spring and summer offer an abundance of flowers that we often wish could stay with us all year long. When we display our framed collages, they remind us of our sweet memories in the garden with our friends.

MATERIALS

- Watercolor paper or cardstock
- Watercolors or paint
- Paintbrush
- Pressed flowers and herbs (see page 12 to learn how)
- Craft glue
- Frame

ROSE, or beach rose (*Rosa rugosa*), grows the most beautiful brightly colored pink flowers, which are delicately yet heavenly scented. Its edible fruits, often called rose hips, are round or oval and range from red to orange. The deeper the color, the riper they are. Rose hips are rich in vitamin C and are one of our favorite plant parts for making teas, herbal honeys, syrups, and glycerites that support our immune system. The fruit also provides food for small animals and birds.

INSTRUCTIONS

1. Paint your paper with the watercolors or paint and allow it to dry.

2. Arrange your pressed flowers and herbs on the paper.

3. When you're happy with your design, carefully glue the flowers and herbs to the paper using a paintbrush.

4. Let dry, then insert the collage into a frame.

Paint your paper to create a background for your collage.

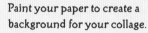

Take your time when creating your design.

MUGWORT
Dream Portal

with Aylén Maquehue

We can connect with the magic of plants by bringing them into our homes. Mugwort, whose Latin name is *Artemisia vulgaris*, is a powerful plant. It can enhance our dreams and help us explore other worlds and our imagination.

MATERIALS

- **Five to seven 12-inch-long stems of mugwort**
- **Natural twine, yarn, or string**
- **Herbs for dreamwork, like chamomile, lavender, rose, and yarrow**
- **Feathers, ribbons, or stones**
- **Scissors**

MUGWORT is a flowering herb widespread across North America. It has been used throughout history as medicine and in food and drinks, and it is lovely in bouquets. Because mugwort spreads so quickly and easily, always foraging for this plant is recommended.

INSTRUCTIONS

1. Line up the stems so their ends are even. Tie them together at the bottom with twine, leaving the spool or ball attached.

2. Bend the mugwort stems to form a circle. Wrap the twine around the mugwort.

3. Wind around a second time to reinforce the shape of the portal.

4. Add additional herbs and decorations, securing with twine.

5. When finished, cut the twine, leaving enough length to hang the portal above your bed and invite sweet dreams.

When you are ready for a new portal, remove any nonbiodegradable elements. Thank the mugwort, and give it back to the earth by composting it or offering it to a fire (with the help of an adult).

Wrap twine around the mugwort circle twice so it keeps its shape.

Decorate your portal with objects that have called to you, brought you joy, or have special meaning.

LEAF PAPER

with Ayo Ngozi

A lot of paper is made from trees (or even better, recycled paper), but did you know that you can make paper from leaves and grass? I use lemongrass, which grows abundantly in my yard, but daylily leaves, iris leaves, sunflower leaves, beach grass, yucca, or any plant that has strong cellulose fibers will work. Because of the materials used, ask for help from an adult in this activity, as needed.

MATERIALS

- Plant material
- Scissors or shears
- Bucket
- Strainer
- Scale
- Large stainless steel pot
- Quart measure
- Rubber gloves
- Safety goggles
- Soda ash (sodium carbonate, also called washing soda; find it in the detergent aisle of grocery and hardware stores)
- Blender
- Plastic bin (a few inches larger than the mould and deckle on all sides)
- 5 x 7-inch mould and deckle (a two-piece screen and frame used in papermaking; can be found in craft stores)
- Sponge
- Craft felt (5 x 7 inches)

Make Your Own Mould and Deckle

Trace a frame onto a piece of paper, then cut it out. Use this as a pattern to cut out a piece of fiberglass or polyester window screening. Staple or tack that piece of screening to the back of the frame to make the mould. For the deckle, line the frame with foam weatherstrip tape. This will prevent paper pulp from leaking out as you are forming sheets.

INSTRUCTIONS

1. If your plant material is freshly harvested (and preferably harvested at the end of its season), let it dry.

2. With scissors or shears, cut the plant material into ½-inch pieces. Fill a bucket with lukewarm water, add the plant pieces, and let them soak for 24 hours.

3. Strain the plant pieces from the water and weigh the plant material. Put it in a stainless steel pot.

4. Add 8 quarts of water for every 1 pound of plant material.

5. Wearing rubber gloves and goggles, add ½ cup of soda ash per pound of plant material to the pot. (Soda ash can cause skin irritation. If you do touch it, rinse it off immediately.)

6. Bring the contents of the pot to a boil, then reduce the heat and simmer for 1 hour. If the plant fibers come apart easily, they're ready for blending. If not, simmer for another 30 minutes and check again.

7. Remove the pot from the heat. Strain the liquid into a bucket. Then rinse the plant fibers with water. Discard the liquid into a sink.

8. Put 2 cups of the rinsed fibers in a blender with enough water to fill it three-fourths of the way. Blend for 30-second intervals until the fibers float In the water and there are no clumps or stringy bits.

9. Pour the contents of the blender into the plastic bin. This is your paper pulp. Repeat as needed with the remaining rinsed fibers.

10. Now you're ready to "pull" a sheet of paper: Lower the mould and deckle into the bin at a 45-degree angle until it is fully submerged and flat at the bottom of the bin. Lift them out of the mixture and shake left to right and back to front, so the fibers interlock and settle on the screen.

Two freshly made sheets of paper

11. Remove the deckle (the empty frame) from the mould. Use a sponge to gently press out the excess water from the paper.

12. Place the felt on top of the wet paper, then flip the paper onto a flat surface, so that the paper is on top of the felt.

13. Dry the wet sheets of paper by hanging them on a clothesline. Remove the felt after the paper has dried.

Plant
GARLANDS

with Molly Meehan Brown

Making garlands is an easy way to invite herbal beauty into your home, learning, or celebratory space and connect with specific plant friends.

MATERIALS

- Scissors
- String, twine, or yarn
- Needle
- Plant material, as desired (herbs, flowers, leaves, pinecones, dried citrus slices, cranberries, popcorn, and so on)

INSTRUCTIONS

1. Cut the string to the desired length of the garland plus several inches. Tie a knot at one end.

2. Thread the opposite end of the string through the eye of the needle. Push the needle through the plant materials, drawing the string through them with care so they do not tear or break.

3. When you're finished adding your materials, remove the needle, knot the end of the string, and trim off any extra.

Cranberries and dried lemons make a festive holiday garland.

Hang your finished garland in a special location.

Flower Tape
BRACELETS

with Malka Roth and Samaria Marley

Make beautiful botanical bracelets with flowers like lilies, peonies, roses, and lilacs for you and your friends.

MATERIALS

- Scissors
- 2-inch-wide masking tape
- Flowers and leaves

INSTRUCTIONS

1. Cut a piece of masking tape slightly longer than your wrist. Wrap it around your wrist sticky-side up, overlapping at the ends, to create the "bracelet." (You may need another set of hands to do this.)

2. Pull the flowers apart and stick the petals and leaves onto the tape. Turn the tape as you work so you cover it all.

Decorate the tape with a variety of colors and textures.

Daisy Chain CROWN

with Molly Meehan Brown

A flower crown is the perfect adornment for special occasions and makes any day feel like a celebration. When you're done wearing it, hang it to dry as a keepsake or memory of the day.

MATERIALS

- Scissors
- Fresh flowers with flexible stems

INSTRUCTIONS

1. Cut the stems to the same length. Begin with two flowers. Wrap the stem of one around the flower of the other. The stem should cross in front of the second flower.

2. Slide the flower to the left with your desired spacing and repeat step 1. As the stems end, add more flowers until you have woven enough length to make a crown.

3. To finish, wrap the last flower around the first flower, forming a circle.

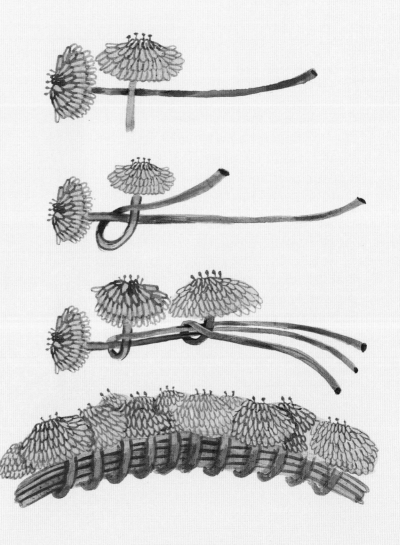

Wildcrafting Code of Ethics

Wildcrafting is the practice of foraging or harvesting plants that were not intentionally grown by humans. You might, for example, wildcraft in a forest or local park with permission. It can be an empowering practice that helps connect us with our home, the land where we live, and the local ecological community, but it requires us to have integrity—a way of being honest and doing what is morally right. There is no strict set of rules here, but it is important to remember that we don't have the right to take whatever we want from the natural world, even if it doesn't technically "belong" to another person.

Foraging for pawpaw fruit

1. Reflect on who you are and your relationship with the land. Reflect on the Indigenous people who have stewarded this land and their guidance on how to be in relationship with it.

2. Consider the wellness of the plants and the local ecosystem. Overharvesting and habitat loss are very real concerns. Wildcraft in ways that help plant communities thrive.

3. We are a community of species, and many other species—animals, insects, microbes—rely on wild plants for their well-being. Harvest when a plant has already produced its seed, or divide and replant. That way, you can help grow new plants.

4. Never harvest based solely on your own desires or needs. The needs of the plants must be considered first.

5. Be sure to correctly identify any plants you are considering harvesting in order to stay safe.

Starting SEEDS

with Rebecca Cecere Seward

Starting seeds is an incredible experience: You get to witness a small seed come to life and become a whole plant. The seeds listed below are "companion plants," which means they help each other grow in the garden. For example, one plant might give off a scent that repels bugs that like to eat the companion plant. Or perhaps the chemical relationship between their roots under the soil helps both plants. Plant them in the same pot or near each other outside, and they will both do better.

Baby seedlings just starting to grow

MATERIALS

- **Craft sticks**
- **Permanent marker**
- **Large bowl**
- **Seed-starting mix**
- **Seed-starting containers, such as paper egg cartons or plastic cups**
- **Pencil or chopstick (optional)**
- **Seeds: lettuce and calendula, tomato and basil, radish and nasturtium, kale and cilantro**
- **Misting spray bottle filled with water**
- **Plastic bags (big enough to hold your seed-starting containers) or plastic wrap**
- **Watering can**
- **Shallow plate(s) or tray(s)**

INSTRUCTIONS

1. Write each plant name and the date on a craft stick with the permanent marker.

2. Fill the large bowl with seed-starting mix. Add water, mixing it in a little bit at a time, until the soil is evenly moist but not sopping wet.

3. Fill them with soil almost all the way to the top.

4. Make a hole in the soil two to three times the size of a seed using a pencil, a chopstick, or your finger. Drop two or three seeds in each hole. (Not every seed will sprout, and later you will pick the best one to plant.)

Tip: Start twice as many seeds as the number of plants you want so you can select the healthiest seedlings when it is time to plant.

5. Sprinkle a little more soil over the top of the seeds. Then gently mist the seeds with water from the spray bottle. Insert your plant markers into the soil.

6. Cover the containers with a plastic bag or plastic wrap. This will keep the seeds warm and humid so they will start to grow.

7. Place the containers in a sunny window and check them every day. Seeds won't sprout without water, so mist the soil whenever it seems dry.

8. Once you see your seedlings poke up out of the soil, remove the plastic covering. Continue to mist with water as needed. When the seedlings are a few inches tall, you can use a watering can to water them. Place shallow plate(s) or tray(s) underneath to catch the excess water.

9. Your seedlings will be ready to go outside when they have grown their "true leaves," meaning they have leaves that look like those of the adult version of the plant, and when the weather is warm enough for them.

10. Set the plants in the shade for a few hours every day, and gradually get them used to being in the sun and wind before transplanting them into outdoor containers or the ground. (Be sure to read your seed packets again for planting instructions.)

CALENDULA, or pot marigold, has orange or yellow flowers and a long growing season in warmer climates. One small plant can produce flowers all year when gently harvested or picked. When you touch the flowers, they feel sticky. The stickiness is a medicinal resin, or the healing part of the plant. Calendula's dried petals can be used to help soothe irritated or sensitive skin and treat minor burns, bruises, or cuts. Natural yellow dyes can also be made from this plant.

Seed
BALLS

with Suzann Stone

Seed balls are combinations of clay, compost, and seeds that let you plant flowers, food, and even trees with one well-aimed throw. You can use a seed ball to beautify a neglected area, a clear-cut piece of land, or even your own backyard, if you have permission to do so.

MATERIALS

- 1 cup powdered red clay
- 2 cups compost or potting soil
- Large bowl
- Spoon
- Seed mix for pollinator-friendly wildflowers native to your area

- Tray or plate, for drying the seed balls
- Container, for storing the seed balls

> **NOTE:** *Work outside or wear a mask to avoid breathing in any of the clay dust.*

INSTRUCTIONS

1. Combine the clay and compost in a large bowl and mix well with a spoon. Add room-temperature water, 1 tablespoon at a time, until you have a clay mixture that holds its shape when you roll it.

2. Pinch off a bit of the clay mixture. It should be no bigger than a quarter and no smaller than a dime in diameter. Take a small pinch of seeds and stick them into the clay mixture, then roll it into a ball. Set the ball on a tray or plate and let air-dry for 1 to 2 days. Repeat to make as many seed balls as you like.

3. Store the seed balls in an open container out of sunlight until you're ready to use. (A closed container will trap moisture and cause the seeds and other microbes to grow.)

TO USE: Plant seed balls by pressing them into soil or by throwing them for added fun.

Dehydrated HARVEST

with Molly Meehan Brown

There are certain times when herbs, vegetables, and fruit are in season, meaning they are ready to eat. A dehydrator is an electric box with a fan that dries food and herbs, allowing you to enjoy what you have grown or obtained from local farmers all year long.

INGREDIENTS

- Herbs, vegetables, or fruit you'd like to dehydrate

NOTE: *For this activity, you'll need a dehydrator. Perhaps you can borrow one from a friend. It can be great to share!*

INSTRUCTIONS

1. Slice your produce. (Ask an adult for help if you need it.) Cut fruits like apples, peaches, and bananas into ¼-inch slices. Cherry tomatoes can be halved, and larger tomatoes will need to be sliced. Herbs can be chopped on their stems.

2. Spread the produce evenly across the dehydrator screens or trays.

3. Set your dehydrator to 125°F (50°C) or, for moisture-rich fruits and vegetables like grapes, cranberries, and zucchini, to 135°F (60°C). Place the screens or trays in the dehydrator. They'll need anywhere from half a day to a couple of days to dehydrate. Fruit is done when it becomes leathery and is no longer sticky. Vegetables are done when they are crisp and hard.

4. Once the food is fully dry, remove it from the screens or trays. Store dehydrated food in glass jars with lids, away from sunlight, heat, and moisture. It will keep for 4 to 12 months.

CHAPTER 5

LISTEN, MOVE, AND REJOICE

Sometimes it's best to take a break.
Sit down and take a listen.
Breathe in, breathe out, become aware
Of the sounds and calls, nature's transmission.

A seed pod can be full and dry,
And when you pick, be sure to hear,
It rattles with full-of-life potential,
Each seed can be heard so clear.

Our instruments are made from plants.
Music is a special kind of plant medicine.
Drums, banjos, berimbau, and flutes,
They help bring alive our rituals and our feelings.

The plants are our ancestors,
They were here long before us.
When we connect to them with our hearts,
If we listen, they will tell us.

Seed
RATTLES

with Molly Meehan Brown

For centuries, plants have been used to make many of our most loved and celebrated musical instruments: guitars, banjos, and drums from wood; flutes from bamboo; and rattles from hollowed-out gourds with seeds inside. In this activity, you will create a seed rattle, which is a percussion instrument used to create rhythm.

MATERIALS

- **Clean, empty plastic bottle or jar with a lid**
- **Masking tape**
- **Acrylic paints or watercolors**
- **¼ cup seeds (dried beans, acorns, or popcorn)**

INSTRUCTIONS

1. Cover the outside of the bottle with tape to create a paintable surface.

2. Use the paints to decorate your rattle with an image or colors that represent the music you would like to play, or paint the plants of the seeds you will be using inside. Let the rattle dry.

3. Place the seeds into the bottle, then screw on the lid tightly.

4. Create rhythms or play along with your favorite songs. Enjoy the sounds of the seeds!

Invite your friends to start a band! Shake your rattle to create a beat while they play along using pumpkins for drums and sticks for drumsticks. Use a sunflower as a microphone to sing along to your favorite songs.

Plant WIND CHIMES

with Molly Meehan Brown

There is nothing quite like being out in the garden and hearing the sound of wind chimes echo through the air. While many are made from metal, they can also be crafted from bamboo and other plant materials.

MATERIALS

- Natural string, twine, or yarn
- Sticks 5 to 10 inches long (fallen from trees)
- Scissors
- Pinecones, acorns, seeds, beads, nuts, bamboo, and plant materials that could produce sound when blowing in the wind
- Stones (in shapes that can be tied and hung by string)

INSTRUCTIONS

1. Tie string to both ends of a stick. The string will create a V-shaped hanger. Allow extra length for adjusting the hanger later.

2. Add more sticks to the hanger, using string as desired to create more rows. Tie on the items you have gathered. Make sure all the items hang freely, staggering the lengths as you like.

3. Hang your plant wind chime in a special location. Adjust the length of the hanger as desired.

Listening
GARDEN

with Molly Meehan Brown

Every place on Earth has its own native pollinators—animals that, in relationship with local trees and plants, have adapted to be able to pollinate those trees and plants. Honeybees, bumblebees, butterflies, and wasps are well-known pollinators, but did you know that birds, bats, ants, lizards, lemurs, and skinks can also be pollinators? In this activity, you will create a pollinator-friendly garden. If you are unable to grow your own pollinator garden, visit any green space with native wildflowers.

MATERIALS

- Paper and pen, for designing your garden
- Sign-making supplies (wood and paint, labels with markers, or whatever you have)
- Potting soil and pots (if you are planting a container garden
- Trowel or shovel
- Pollinator-friendly native seeds, seedlings, or plants
- Watering can or hose

Listen to the pollinators as they visit. Do they buzz, chirp, or hum? Where is the sound coming from—perhaps the flapping of their wings?

Native Pollinator Gardens

Our food, forests, prairies, and plant life worldwide depend on pollinators for survival. Planting a pollinator garden can be a great way to provide habitat and food for these important allies. Grow your plants from seeds, or buy them at local plant sales or nurseries. Be sure they do not spray with chemicals that could harm the pollinators visiting your garden.

INSTRUCTIONS

1. Select and prepare a space based on the needs of the plants you intend to grow, like sunlight, soil conditions, and how big the plants will become. Draw a plan for which plant will go where.

2. Create signs to identify your plants. You might paint their names on pieces of wood or use a permanent marker to write on small metal labels you can stick in the soil.

3. If you are planting a container garden, mix your potting soil with enough water so that it feels moist but is not sopping wet. Use it to fill your pots. If you're planting in the ground, water the garden soil.

4. Using a trowel or shovel, dig holes, then plant your seeds, seedlings, or plants at the recommended depth and distance.

5. Give your seeds or plants a deep soak with a watering can or hose.

6. Make sure your garden receives the right amount of water, whether by rain or watering, especially in the first few weeks after planting. (You will need to water plants in containers more often than ones planted in the ground.)

7. As your plants grow and begin to flower, your garden will be full of life. It can be a wonderful place to relax and observe who comes to visit and hear all the sounds of these important pollinators at work.

Rhythms and Cycles

Rhythms and cycles are woven throughout nature. They teach us how to move with plants. Whether you live in a place with four seasons or a tropical one where it is warm all year round, begin to pay attention to the rhythms and cycles around you. Notice:

THE RHYTHMS OF YOUR BODY, such as when you sleep, when you wake up, and when you get hungry. Do the physical needs of your body happen at the same time every day?

THE RHYTHMS OF THE MOON, passing through phases from the new moon to a full moon every month

THE RHYTHMS OF THE DAYS, with almost equal light and darkness near the equator. But in the global north and south, there are periods of longer light or longer darkness, depending on the time of year.

THE RHYTHMS OF FRUIT, ripening in cycles year after year

THE RHYTHMS OF TREES, like when the leaves drop off deciduous trees, or when certain birds come to visit

THE RHYTHMS OF THE OCEAN, with tides rising and falling throughout the day

Have you noticed these rhythms? What other natural rhythms have you noticed? How does climate change affect these rhythms?

Ideally we harvest and create plant preparations when plants are in their fullest expression, and we can observe this by learning their rhythms.

SPRING

We observe the earth beginning to exhale. All the leaves and aerial parts of the plants start to come out.

SUMMER

The exhale expands into a full breath! We see lush green leaves, an abundance of plants, the harvest, and plant reproduction, with seed setting in toward the end of summer. It is best to harvest leaves before the plants' energy has moved toward reproduction and seed setting later.

FALL

The earth begins to inhale, pulling its energy inward. Leaves begin to fall, and plants begin to slowly go to sleep for winter. Late fall into early winter after a couple of frosts can be a great time to harvest certain roots.

WINTER

Pausing. The energy is underground in the roots of the plants, resting until it reaches the full exhale.

MONTHLY

Each month a similar rhythm occurs. During the new moon, the energy of the plants goes down into the roots. During the full moon, the energy is pulled up into the aerial parts, making that an ideal time to make plant preparations with those parts. Of course, this is not always possible, and that's okay! But it is important to be aware of these cycles.

Nature
POEM

with Molly Meehan Brown

One fun way to record your nature observations is to write a poem.
Poetry is writing that brings your creativity, your experiences,
or even your imagination to life! You can focus on the specific
words you use and the sounds or rhythm they create.

MATERIALS

- **Paper or a notepad**
- **Pen or pencil**

INSTRUCTIONS

1. Sit outdoors in a favorite comfortable place. If you can't go outdoors, find a window where you can look out at the sky, a tree, or another part of nature, or sit near a plant or an animal that lives inside your house. Notice how you're feeling as you look around.

   - What is making you happy?

   - What do you feel on your skin?

   - Are you smelling anything?

   - What's the weather like?

   - What is the light like?

   - What season is it?

   - What's the time of day?

   - How are all these things making you feel inside?

2. As words or phrases pop into your head, write them down. Write as many lines as you like. Now see if you can put them together into a poem.

3. Read your poem aloud to share it with your friends and family. Invite all of them to join in and write their own nature poem!

CHAPTER 6

community CONSTELLATION

Herbs hold our stories, our traditions,
our families, our communities, our cultural
practices, and our art.

Herbs weave relationships, provide rituals,
and sit at the center of our celebrations.

Plants are a great way to bring
community together. Plants themselves
live in community—with other plants,
trees, minerals, fungi, and microbes in their
environment—and can teach us how to build
our own community.

Little Herbalist
SAVES THE WORLD!

with Susan and Isabella Leopold

Isabella enjoys cooking and helping in the garden. She has accompanied her mom to many herbal gatherings. One day, she asked if she could host her own.

MATERIALS

- **Your creativity and imagination**
- **Paper**
- **Pencil**
- **Art supplies**

INSTRUCTIONS

1. Come up with a name for your gathering, a logo or artwork to decorate your invitation, and a mission statement (a sentence or two describing your goals).

2. Begin working on all the details for your event so you can create a flyer to advertise it. Like a party invitation, the flyer lists details of what day, where, the time, and any instructions.

3. Make a list of activities you would like to do at your gathering. Isabella decided on a plant walk to identify 10 plants, making elderberry syrup over an outdoor fire, and a botany class (*botany* is another word for studying or learning about

plants). You might want to pick some of your favorite activities from this book.

4. For Isabella's gathering, she had to decide who would be leading the walk and the classes. She also made a list of materials and supplies that would be needed. You will want to do the same.

5. Now that all the details are planned, make the flyer. Share your flyer with friends and family. (Ask an adult for help if you need or want it.)

6. Enjoy your herbal community gathering!

10 Ways to Build Your Community

1. Host an herbal potluck or tea party with your friends.

2. Organize a storytelling time in your community. Listen to people share the ways in which they have been in relationships with plants.

3. Get together with your friends and share your favorite books and plants.

4. Host a plant or seed swap.

5. Organize a group to help rehome plants that may be losing their habitat due to development. (Always ask an adult to help you get proper permission before going onto land that is being developed.)

6. Host an herbal craft activity or fair.

7. Organize an herbal gathering in your community (see facing page).

8. Create herbal self-care kits with friends and family to donate to a local mutual aid project.

9. Grow an herb garden at home or with friends at a community garden.

10. Join a plant network such as United Plant Savers.

Sourcing Herbs

As we build our relationships with herbs, it's important to consider where to get them. If you have access to a yard, a spot in a local community garden, or even space for some pots, you can easily grow your own.

We love getting our seeds from local community seed exchanges and garden clubs. Once we begin growing an herb, we save the seeds for our own garden and give them to members of our community.

For plants, we head to local nurseries and plant sales that take place in the spring.

If you are purchasing dried herbs, I recommend buying from local herbalists, small apothecaries, and farms. Food co-ops, community herbal groups or education centers, and health food stores are also good options. Many local, regional, and ethical herb farms can be found online. So can small-scale herbal apothecaries and bulk sellers who support local farms and sustainable practices.

Processing Herbs

After we harvest herbs, we often process or prepare them for making herbal recipes. There are many beautiful cultural tools, practices, and traditions for how to do this, but the most basic methods are explained here.

CLEAN

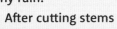

When working with the aerial (aboveground) parts of the plant, like stems, leaves, flowers, fruit, or seeds, harvest at least a few days after any rain.

After cutting stems or sprigs, I gently shake them so that any flying insects fly away, then I check that there are no other insects. While washing is not necessary, some people prefer this practice. If you do, too, make sure to dry the herbs well so mold does not grow.

WILT

Freshly harvested plants have a very high water content. For certain preparations, especially in oils, you will need to reduce the amount of water by wilting. To do this, tie a few stems together and hang them, or lay the plant material out on a clean table, screen, or baking sheet for a day. They will not be fully dry, but a significant amount of the water content will have evaporated.

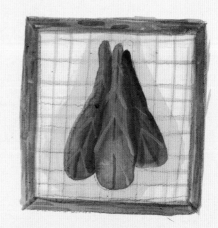

DRY

Humans have been drying herbs for thousands of years to preserve them for future use.

I have a string tied across my kitchen window with a few clothespins, and I'll hang herb bundles of three to five stalks tied together up there before I process them further for storage.

A dehydrator is another way to dry herbs if you have access to one. Although fun and effective, dehydrators are not often necessary.

GARBLE

Garbling is a fancy word for stripping dried leaves from their stems. Hold the top of the stalk or stem securely in one hand. With the thumb and index finger of your other hand, grab the stalk and run those fingers down, which will easily remove the leaves. Afterward, be sure to pick out any stems that may have snuck in.

STORE

I like to store dried herbs in clean recycled glass jars with lids. Ideally you want to store herbs out of direct sunlight, without extreme heat or cold, and with as little humidity as possible.

Consent and Gratitude

The herbs and the earth are abundant! That said, they do not exist solely for our use. We have a responsibility to take care of our world, including the plants. When we do things like sit with plants, grow plants, harvest them, or prepare food or remedies from them, it is important that we ask them for permission and give them our thanks.

Ask permission. Before harvesting, ask the plant for permission. Listen, connect to the plant, and you will know. Sometimes it's just a small feeling in your body saying, *Yes, you can pick me,* or, *No, leave me be, please!*

Give thanks. When a plant offers itself for our food or medicine, we can express our gratitude to the plant, to Earth, to the Creator, and to our ancestors. In fact, we can practice gratitude whether or not we harvest the plant. We can also honor the plants by adding any bits of them that are left over to our compost, in this way returning them to their soil.

Asking for consent and practicing gratitude help us remember that good herbalism, healing, and right relationship cannot be rushed. Take all the time you need to learn from the plants. Your goal as an herbalist is not to "use" the plants but to learn to work together with them.

Herbalists as Caretakers

As stewards, or caretakers, we should protect plants that grow in small numbers or whose habitat is being threatened. This means not using or harvesting them. It also means using invasive species—plants that do not normally grow where you found them—whenever we can. There is research being done now on harvesting invasive species to use for medicine. There are so many ways to be good stewards as plant people!

Many leaders in our communities have been teaching what it means to be good stewards and in right relationship with the plants. The Seed, Soil + Spirit School is a great example. This school uplifts the histories, stories, and relationships of plant medicine by bringing together diverse herbalists and thinkers to create programs that help people be in right relationship with the land and plants.

Another resource is United Plant Savers. This organization's mission is to protect native medicinal plants, fungi, and their habitats while ensuring renewable populations for generations to come. They have created bioregional lists of plants that are at risk for the United States and beyond. Check out the resources on page 101 to learn more about ethical wildcrafting organizations.

Community of Contributors

KATE BACKWINKEL started Mama Bears Elderberries in 2019 and became the first and only licensed elderberry producer in Maryland. Expanding to native elder growth and production, they planted an initial 200 plants in 2020 and are now the largest-known elder grower in Maryland. Mama Bears focuses on producing high-quality elderberry syrups using local ingredients, and Kate is passionate about sharing knowledge on elderberry production, herbalism, and holistic health and supporting local communities and farms.

ALDA COOK CAMPBELL is a traditional herbalist, keeper of Afro Costa Rican foodways, and mother and grandmother. Born and raised by her grandmother Miss Edith in the small fishing village of Manzanillo in the Caribe Sur of Costa Rica, Alda still visits the same plants taught to her by her grandmother. She teaches, leads plant walks, and tends her family and community with her plant remedy knowledge and healing cooking.

ZENOVIA D'ARIENZO is a mother, creator, business owner, teacher, and chef. She was born on the island of Trinidad, spent her childhood in T&T (Trinidad and Tobago), then migrated to the United States. Her culture, she says, made her who she is today, and she is grateful to have been taught by her elders and to be able to know, teach, and share a little bit of home with others.

SUMI DUTTA is a queer desi writer, neighborhood herbalist, and radical facilitator from Durham, North Carolina. She runs a creative healing and facilitation practice called sumistreet. She is a cofounder of the Durham Community Apothecary, an herbal mutual aid project that redistributes free and low-cost herbal medicine.

GEOFFREY EDWARDS is a practitioner and educator whose art-centered practice integrates art therapy, acupuncture, and herbal medicine. He is owner of Grain & Pestle, an herb apothecary, treatment space, and art studio based in Detroit, Michigan. Grain & Pestle is a receptacle for the active convergence of the grains of life: healing, creativity, community, and learning.

ARVOLYN HILL (she/her) is an outdoor educator and herbalist. She is the manager of the Everett Children's Adventure Garden, a children's garden within the New York Botanical Garden in the Bronx. There she teaches kids from toddler to teenager about plants. She is also a community herbalist with an apothecary called Gold Feather Shop. In her spare time, Arvolyn likes to DJ, hula hoop, and garden in her community garden in Harlem, New York.

MASON HUTCHISON is the founder of HerbRally, a website that promotes herbalism education and events. HerbRally is home to a daily herbal podcast, a YouTube channel, tons of plant monographs, and a whole lot more. He is a proud husband and father; an avid basketball, chess, and table tennis player; a spring-water gatherer; and an enthusiast in the art of frugal nutrition.

NAMITA KULKARNI is an Indian yoga teacher, a writer, and an artist who has been teaching yoga for 11 years in four countries, primarily India. She was a full-time artist before she began teaching yoga professionally and now indulges in both of these passions—art and teaching yoga—and their synergy.

SUSAN LEOPOLD is the executive director of United Plant Savers, a nonprofit dedicated to native medicinal plant conservation. Her daughter Isabella Luna created the Little Herbalist Saves the World! event (see page 90).

AYLÉN MAQUEHUE (she/they) is a Queer, Brazilian-born, Mapuche/mixed herbalist currently based on the Piscataway land also known as Baltimore, Maryland, where they grow plants, formulate herbal medicines, and explore the world of fermentation. She is the founder of Ruka Healing House, offering

clinical herbal services and workshops that center QT+ and BIPOC folks and focus on restoring our kinship with plants and land. They are enthusiastic about organizing events and knowledge shares and working toward collective healing and liberation. Aylén's work as an herbalist is based on the premise that healing is activism, knowledge belongs to everyone, and the plants can guide the path to liberation. Chaltumay!

SAMARIA MARLEY is an herbalist, a farmer, a somatic practitioner, and an artist. She is the cofounder of the DC Mutual Aid Apothecary, an organization that mobilizes herbalists, herbal enthusiasts, farmers, and holistic health practitioners in the metropolitan Washington region. Samaria also manages a small-scale herb farm in Brandywine, Maryland, called Junipers Garden.

MADISON McCOY is the founder of Of Earth and Sea, a liminal space tasked with the mission of building a more equitable world by equipping individuals with generative conflict transformation tools,

deep self-awareness, and a reverence for the earth and her many blessings and lessons. Madison is a certified personal transformation facilitator and a flower essence practitioner, an oracle card reader, a mindfulness teacher, and a nature school educator. She holds a degree in community conflict transformation from George Mason University. She uses a whole-self and trauma-informed approach to guide individuals in accessing their own deep well of healing, transformation, and imaginative power. She currently lives on a farm outside of Washington, DC, with her partner and two tortoises.

MARYSIA MIERNOWSKA is a teacher, an author, an Earth activist, a green witch, a folk herbalist, founder of the School of the Sacred Wild, and a healer rooted in the wise woman tradition of healing. A multilingual and multicultural devotee of Mother Earth, Marysia has spent her life traveling, learning, and sharing different regenerative ways of tending to the Earth, healing land, and healing people. Born in Poland, she carries with her a lineage of European folk herbalism and her training and personal experience with the plants and connection to Earth. Marysia honors plants as sentient beings, elders, healers, and teachers.

AYO NGOZI is an herbalist, a writer, an artist, and a mother. A graduate of the Maryland University of Integrative Health, she is a guest instructor and an adviser to several herbal schools and programs in the United States and abroad. Ayo lives and works on Yamacraw land (Savannah, Georgia).

LUPO PASSERO is a community herbalist and the director of Twin Star School of Herbal & Energetic Studies (twinstsrtribe.com). She brings with her over 25 years of knowledge, intimate relationships, and understanding of the plants and flower essences as a mother, teacher, and green

witch. Lupo has had the honor to learn from many teachers and lineages of plant medicine throughout Europe and Central America, she centers and draws deeply upon her own Italian and Irish ancestral knowledge. She has taught The Art of Flower Essence Therapy course since the early 2000s and offers flower essence practitioner trainings annually in the US and abroad.

IRLANDA "LANDIS" PULIDO is a Queer-Chicane-Indigene who honors their people from Mexico as they walk with permission on these sacred lands. They are a graduate of the University of California

at Santa Cruz, a teaching artist, a community organizer, and a healing justice practitioner with offerings of bodywork, plant medicine, and (w)holistic practices. They believe in bringing the breath, movement, and healing into the arts and creative space to invite wholeness, imagination, and joy. They are forever grateful for their community learning and growing on Piscataway, Tongva, and Tiwa/Ute lands. Gracias.

ANGELA RAHIM is an herbalist, a doula, and a permaculturist from Baltimore, Maryland. She is the mother of eight children, a preschool teacher, and an avid gardener. She is the author of several books, including *Sam: The Junior Herbalist*. She can be found teaching herbalism to children around the world and going to Cavaliers games with her husband, Burheem, in her free time.

TONI ROBERTS is a homeschool mom based in southern Maryland. She encourages her children to stay close to nature to learn many of life's valuable lessons.

She believes that in a world where we are less connected, the most revolutionary thing we can do is connect to the earth and our communities. When she's not spending time with family, Toni also supports her community through herbal medicine making, birthwork, yoga, meditation, energy work, and women's healing circles.

MALKA ROTH (she/her) is an educator, herbalist, organizer, and cofounder of the DC Mutual Aid Apothecary. She organizes locally in DC and in the national landscape. Malka's work is profoundly influenced by abolitionism, her queer and Jewish identities, and an enduring conviction that new worlds are possible.

REBECCA CECERE SEWARD is a flower farmer, homesteader, and mother growing and living in southern Maryland. She shares her life with her human family, dogs, cats, goats, sheep, ducks, chickens, a whole lot of plants, and all the wild creatures who come and go from the land she calls home.

SUZANNA STONE is an herbalist and a teacher with more than 20 years of experience in clinical and energetic herbalism. Suzanna was raised with a strong connection to plant medicine and whole foods, which provided the foundation for her

life's work. In 2008 she founded Owlcraft Healing Ways, an outdoor herb school focused not only on teaching the skills and knowledge necessary to be an herbalist but also on deepening engagements with the land, the self, and the community. Based in rural central Virginia, Suzanna offers a variety of herbal apprenticeships, weekend programs, and herb camps for children as well as a clinical practice.

The **DC MUTUAL AID APOTHECARY** (DCMA) is a volunteer-led mutual aid organization cofounded in 2020 by Malka Roth and Samaria Marley as a response to COVID-19. For the past three years DCMA has provided free, nonalcoholic herbal medicine, education, and space for community building and community care for people of all ages and backgrounds. Their mission is to connect their community to accessible plant medicine and education, reconnect to ancestral plant knowledge, and distribute herbal products to underresourced communities across the city.

Fifty percent of the proceeds from this book are committed to the DC Mutual Aid Apothecary and the essential work they are carrying on in their community.

Gratitude from Molly

Gratitude at first to Divine Interconnectedness. As a settler of Irish descent, I extend gratitude to my own ancestors. I also acknowledge and am deeply grateful to the land and the peoples whose land I have grown up on, the land stewarded and unceded by the Piscataway community, now called Maryland. This land has been my first teacher and has held many of the most fruitful connections and relationships with both plants and people that I have had in my life.

I acknowledge that truly all of my knowledge has come from others. Thus, I could never write this book alone. While I deeply love plants and they are some of my closest relations, in my heart I live where people and plants come together in relationship and community. First and foremost, I have learned from the land and the plants themselves. I am thankful to those who taught me to actually sit, listen, and be with the plants.

My own ancestral lineage goes back primarily to Ireland as well the Czech Republic. My paternal lineage is one of farmers before and even after reaching the United States during the Irish Potato Famine.

I learned first from my family. I have gratitude for my grandmother Gertrude, who cultivated relationship and family and lived faith and love daily. I have gratitude for the way I was raised by BL, a chef, and Kathleen, an educator and gardener, who insisted that instead of screens we use our imaginations and go outside, into the woods or the neighborhood. My parents worked so hard and sacrificed so much for the opportunities we received. I have gratitude for my children, my daily teachers. I have gratitude for the land that holds our family as well as all those who come to explore and learn in community on our farm. I am so thankful for this land as our teacher and our container.

I am thankful for Javier, my beloved, for passing on the skills of patience, of showing up, of gentle steady care, and all you model for myself and for our children.

I am thankful to our children's paternal grandparents, John and Celedonia,

My great-great-grandfather, a farmer, immigrated to the United States in 1901.

My family's home in Ballysadare, County Sligo, Ireland. Over four generations of Meehans lived here.

chocolate farmers and keepers of Afro Costa Rican foodways, who modeled thinking ahead for us future generations by sowing seeds that would bear fruit for the future.

A deep bow of gratitude to Storey Publishing, both for this opportunity as well as for modeling moving at the speed of life and allowing the time for this book to come into fruition. Thank you to the plants and to all my mentors, friends, colleagues, and community for showing up, for believing, for being so generous with your time, knowledge, joy, and trust. To Erika, thank you for being the glue that keeps it all together for us! Thanks also to all of my teachers, many (but not all) of whom have helped write this book. To every single person who teaches with Wild Ginger Community Herbal Center and Kids Herbalism, I love you and am so thankful for you. Thank you to my herbal teachers and those who have taught me most about being in relationship: Padi Blas Martinez, Kat Maier, John Finch, José from Finca Andar, Miguel, Alda and Luba Cook Campbell, the entire Moreno family . . . the list goes on. To Richael Faithful, for being such an incredible model, mentor, and teacher in community and relationship, you are such a gift; thank you. To Ayo Ngozi, Karen Culpepper, Geo Edwards, Lupo Passero, Yuma Bellomee, Oliva Fite, Holly Poole Kavana, Ellenie Cruz, Lacey Walker, Madison McCoy, Muneera Fontaina, Malika Hook Muhammad, Aylén Maquehue, Suzanna Stone, Samaria Marley, and Malka Roth, and all those unnamed, it is the honor of my life and such a gift to work and learn from each of you. I love y'all.

My hope is that I can do this book and the community it serves justice, and that it is helpful in the way it is meant to be. I do not offer hard truths here; in fact, the beauty and strength of herbalism is that it is a practice in relationship with the people and communities who have evolved alongside one another. Herbalism, therefore, is a direct reflection of each community and lineage, and that exists in an expanse of unique practices that differ across communities and cultures.

Each contributor here is someone I deeply respect and honor in our herbal community, and to each one of them I am so grateful for the generosity of the time, care, knowledge, and skills they have shared here.

Both the plants as well as contributors in this book are, to me, models of the idea that what happens at even the smallest level is a reflection of what is and can happen on the larger scale. Where we direct our attention will expand. When we care for and nurture a plant, a garden, a skill, or a relationship or community, it will be nourished and thrive. Personal or small-scale community work and small actions can affect the whole, and the contributors to this book are all through example being in right relationship with themselves, the plants, and Earth and with community. I admire their commitment to bringing each other along as we learn and grow.

Each one of these people also engages in important community-rooted herbal work, and I invite you to learn more about their exciting projects. I admire their work deeply; to be in community and herbal work with many of these people is truly the honor of my life. We are excited for this platform to lift up the important work they are doing in their communities.

Last, I also want to acknowledge and extend gratitude for the fun that was had through all of the activities in the creation of this book. I hope that spirit is felt and expanded upon.

Resources

BOTANY AND PLANT IDENTIFICATION

Botany Every Day
https://botanyeveryday.com

CONSERVATION AND ETHICAL WILDCRAFTING

Alexis Nikole
https://instagram.com /blackforager
https://patreon.com/blackforager

Foraging teacher and environmental science enthusiast

Seed, Soil + Spirit School
https://seedsoilspirit.com

United Plant Savers
https://unitedplantsavers.org

For the research, education, and conservation of native medicinal plants, fungi, and their habitat

HERBAL EDUCATION

HerbRally
https://herbrally.com

Providing a directory of herbal events around the United States and beyond, an energetic podcast, plant monographs, and so much more

Kids Herbalism
www.kidsherbalism.com

Online global community with brand-new weekly classes in herbalism, cooking, gardening, and nurturing relationships with nature for kids

HERBS AND HERBAL SUPPLIES

Avena Botanicals
https://avenabotanicals.com

Gold Feather Shop
https://goldfeathershop.com

Healing Spirits Herb Farm
https://healingspiritsherbfarm .com

Herb Pharm
https://herb-pharm.com

Junipers Garden
https://junipersgarden.org

Mama Bears Elderberries
https://mamabearselderberries .com

Mountain Rose Herbs
https://mountainroseherbs.com

Sacred Vibes Apothecary
https://sacredvibeshealing.com

Zach Woods Herb Farm
www.zackwoodsherbs.com

SEEDS

Strictly Medicinal Seeds
https://strictlymedicinalseeds .com

Truelove Seeds
https://trueloveseeds.com

Index

A

alfalfa seeds, sprouting, 20–21
apples
  Apple-Pear Topping, 54
  Dehydrated Harvest, 79

B

bananas
  Dehydrated Harvest, 79
  Rundown Stew, 40
basil
  in food recipes, 38–39
  growing, 18–19, 22, 76
bee balm facts, 42
beeswax, 56, 57
berries
  Berry and Greens Salad, 36
  Blackberry Ink and
    Twig Pen, 16–17
  Dehydrated Harvest, 79
  Elderberry Herbal Syrup, 51
  Elderberry Propagation,
    24–25
  Fairy Berry Tea, 29
  Party Punch, 30
  Pistachio–Goji Berry
    Chocolate, 43
  Plant Garlands, 72
  Wild Berry Crumble, 46–47
blackberries, 4
  Blackberry Ink and
    Twig Pen, 16–17
  Wild Berry Crumble, 46–47
borage, 34, 65
Botanical Illustration, 14–15
Bracelets, Flower Tape, 73

C

calendula
  facts, 77
  growing, 76–77
  Ice Cubes, 34
cardamom
  Elderberry Herbal Syrup, 51
  facts, 29
  Fairy Berry Tea, 29
Cards and Invitations,
  Fresh Herb 65
carrots
  growing, 18–19
  Rundown Stew, 40
catnip, 4, 42
cayenne, 4, 32
chamomile, 4, 7, 49
  Ice Pops, 42
  Mugwort Dream
    Portal, 68–69
chickweed
  Chickweed Pesto, 39
  facts, 39
chives, growing, 22
chocolate
  with peppermint, 58, 59
  Pistachio–Goji Berry
    Chocolate, 43
cilantro, 27, 33
  Chickweed Pesto, 39
  growing, 76
  Zucchini Fritters, 37
cinnamon, 4–5
  Elderberry Herbal Syrup, 51
  facts, 45
  in food recipes, 44–45,
    46–47, 54
cocoa butter
  Lemon Balm Lip Balm, 56

Pistachio–Goji Berry
  Chocolate, 43
Coconut Drops, 44–45
Collage, Pressed Flower, 66–67
Color Wheel, Herbal, 11
community
  building, 89–91
  of contributors, 95–98
  gardens, 3
  local ecological
    community, 75
  service, 41
cranberries
  Dehydrated Harvest, 79
  Plant Garlands, 72
curry, 29, 33, 64

D

Daisy Chain Crown, 74
dandelion, 4, 74
dehydrators
  Dehydrated Harvest, 79
  drying herbs, 93
  making kale chips, 33
dill
  Botanical Illustration, 14–15
  facts, 15
  in food recipes, 33, 37, 42
drawing
  Blackberry Ink and
    Twig Pen, 16–17
  Botanical Illustration, 14–15
  designing a garden, 84–85
  taking time to observe, 5
Dream Portal, Mugwort, 68–69
dyes for fabric
  calendula, 77
  how to tie-dye, 64
  Natural Dye with
    Turmeric, 62–64

E

elderberries
    Elderberry Herbal Syrup, 51
    Fairy Berry Tea, 29
    how to identify elder
        shrubs, 47
    Simple Elderberry
        Propagation, 24–25
    Wild Berry Crumble, 46–47

F

fennel
    Herbal Pizzas, 38
    Ice Pops, 42
flowers
    Botanical Illustration, 14–15
    Daisy Chain Crown, 74
    edible flowers in recipes,
        30–31, 34, and 42
    Fairy Berry Tea, 29
    Flower Tape Bracelets, 73
    Herbal Color Wheel, 11
    Nature Mandala, 8
    in notecards, 65
    Plant Press and
        Herbarium, 12–13
    Pressed Flower
        Collage, 66–67
frittata and fritters, 37

G

Garlands, Plant, 72
garlic
    Chickweed Pesto, 39
    Fire Cider Oxymel, 32
    Rundown Stew, 40
    Vegetable Frittata, 37
ginger, 4
    Apple-Pear Topping, 54
    beer, 30
    facts, 32
    Fire Cider Oxymel, 32

Kale Chips, 33
glycerite, 66
    Peppermint Glycerite, 58
goji berries
    Pistachio–Goji Berry
        Chocolate, 43
growing herbs and veggies
    Glass Jar Herb Garden, 22
    How to Sprout, 20–21
    No-Waste Kitchen
        Gardening, 18–19
    Simple Elderberry
        Propagation, 24–25
    Starting Seeds, 76–77

H

hawthorn, 4, 53
herbalism and lineage, 41
herbarium, 12–13
hibiscus flowers, 4, 53
    Edible Flower Ice Cubes, 34
    Elderberry Herbal Syrup, 51
    facts, 34
    Fairy Berry Tea, 29
    Party Punch, 30
horseradish, 32

I

ice
    botanical ice art, 30–31
    Ice Pops, 42

J

jalapeño, 32
journaling, 5

K

kale
    Chickweed Pesto, 39
    growing, 76

Spiced Turmeric Kale
    Chips, 33
Vegetable Frittata, 37

L

labeling your remedies, 59
lavender, 3–4, 7, 49, 53
    facts, 31
    in food recipes, 30–31, 34, 42
    Kitchen Wreath, 55
    Mugwort Dream Portal, 68
Leaf Paper, 70–71
lemon balm, 4
    Ice Pops, 42
    Lemon Balm Lip Balm, 56
    Tummy Trouble Tea, 52
lemongrass in leaf paper, 70
lemons, 4
    Chickweed Pesto, 39
    Fire Cider Oxymel, 32
    lemonade with lavender, 31
    Plant Garlands, 72
    Wild Berry Crumble, 46–47
licorice, 4, 38
Lip Balm, 56

M

Mandala, Nature, 8–9
marshmallow, 4, 61
Meditation, Garden, 10
mint, 4–5
    in beverages, 29, 30–31
    Botanical Illustration, 14–15
    facts, 14
    growing in a glass jar, 22
    Ice Pops, 42
    Peppermint Glycerite, 58–59
    spearmint, 4, 29
mist formula, 50
monarda, 7, 42
mould and deckle,
    how to make, 70

mugwort
  facts, 68
  Mugwort Dream
    Portal, 68–69
mullein, 4, 61

N

nettle, 4
  facts, 52
  stinging nettles, 61
  Tummy Trouble Tea, 52
nutmeg
  Apple-Pear Topping, 54
  Coconut Drops, 44–45
  facts, 45

O

oregano, 1
  facts, 22
  growing, 22
  Herbal Pizzas, 38
Oxymel, Fire Cider, 32

P

pansy
  Botanical Illustration, 14–15
  facts, 14
parsley, growing, 22
passionflower, 4, 42
peach
  Dehydrated Harvest, 79
  leaf, 4
pears, 54
peppermint, 49
  facts, 59
  Peppermint Glycerite, 58–59
pesto, 38–39
photosynthesis, 2

pine
  cones, 72, 83
  facts, 57
  needles, 57
  pine nuts, 39
Pistachio–Goji Berry
  Chocolate, 43
Pizza, Decorative Herbal, 38
plant journey, 5
plant names (scientific
  or botanical), 3
Plant Press and
  Herbarium, 12–13
poetry, 7
  Nature Poem, 88
pollinators, 2, 7, 31
  Listening Garden, 84–85
  native pollinator gardens, 85
propagation, 24–25

R

raspberries, 4
  Berry and Greens Salad, 36
rhythms and cycles, 86–87
rose
  Botanical Illustration, 14–15
  Edible Flower Ice Cubes, 34
  facts, 15
  Fairy Berry Tea, 29
  Flower Tape Bracelets, 73
  Mugwort Dream
    Portal, 68–69
rose hips, 51, 53, 66
rosemary, 1, 49, 65
  drying herbs, 4–5
  facts, 50
  Herbal Pizzas, 38
  Kitchen Wreath, 55
  Rosemary Water Mist, 50

S

sage, 4, 7
  Kitchen Wreath, 55
salad
  Berry and Greens Salad, 36
  How to Sprout, 20
salves, 1, 59
  Evergreen Salve, 57
scallions, growing, 18–19
seeds, 1–2, 4
  fennel seeds, 38
  How to Sprout, 20–21
  pollinator gardens, 84–85
  Seed Balls, 78
  Seed Rattles, 82
  sources for, 92
  Starting Seeds, 76–77
  sunflower seeds, 39
shiitake mushrooms, 4
shiso, 38–39
slippery elm, 4–5
spearmint, 4
  Fairy Berry Tea, 29
sprouting alfalfa seeds, 20–21
Stew, Rundown, 40
sunflower seeds, 39
Syrup, Elderberry Herbal, 51

T

tea
  Fairy Berry Tea, 29
  Tummy Trouble Tea, 52
thyme, 1–2, 5
  Evergreen Salve, 57
  facts, 40
  in food recipes, 38, 40, 42
  growing, 22
  Kitchen Wreath, 55
tomatoes
  Dehydrated Harvest, 79

growing, 76
Herbal Pizzas, 38
tulsi, 38
turmeric, 4, 29
facts, 64
Fire Cider Oxymel, 32
Natural Dye with
Turmeric, 62–64
Party Punch, 30–31
Spiced Turmeric Kale Chips, 33
twig pen, 16–17

V

vegetable glycerin, 58
vegetable recipes
Dehydrated Harvest, 79
Herbal Pizzas, 38
Rundown Stew, 40
Vegetable Frittata, 37
Zucchini Fritters, 37

W

walnuts, 53
Chickweed Pesto, 39
Wild Ginger Community
Herbal Center, 28, 100
Wildcrafting Code of Ethics, 75
Wind Chimes, Plant, 83
Wreath, Kitchen, 55

Z

zucchini
drying, 79
Zucchini Fritters, 37

METRIC CONVERSIONS

Unless you have finely calibrated measuring equipment, conversions between US and metric measurements will be somewhat inexact. It's important to convert the measurements for all of the ingredients in a recipe to maintain the same proportions as the original.

WEIGHT		
To convert	to	multiply
ounces	grams	ounces by 28.35
pounds	grams	pounds by 453.5
pounds	kilograms	pounds by 0.45

VOLUME		
To convert	to	multiply
teaspoons	milliliters	teaspoons by 4.93
tablespoons	milliliters	tablespoons by 14.79
cups	milliliters	cups by 236.59
cups	liters	cups by 0.24

LENGTH		
To convert	to	multiply
inches	centimeters	inches by 2.54

Raise Nature-Loving Kids with More Books from Storey

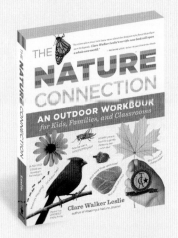

The Nature Connection
by Clare Walker Leslie

Artist Clare Walker Leslie shows kids how to experience nature with all five senses through inspiring activities such as sketching wildlife, observing the constellations, collecting leaves, keeping a weather journal, and watching bird migrations.

Nature's Art Box
by Laura C. Martin

Kids will love these 65 projects that can be made with found materials, including mixing paint from flower blossoms, molding elf-sized furniture from clay, creating twig baskets, and so much more!

Put on Your Owl Eyes
by Devin Franklin

This interactive guide shows kids how to observe and record the sounds, sights, smells, and patterns they find in nature. Learn the Six Arts of Tracking, create a habitat map, walk in silence like a fox, master the basics of bird language, and much more. Includes prompts and spaces for journaling, map-making, and observational tracking.